Difficult Times,
Encouraging Words

James T. Draper, Jr.

CrossBooks™
1663 Liberty Drive
Bloomington, IN 47403
www.crossbooks.com
Phone: 1-866-879-0502

©2009 James T. Draper, Jr.. All rights reserved.

No part of this book may be reproduced, stored in a retrieval system, or transmitted by any means without the written permission of the author.

First published by CrossBooks 6/11/2009

ISBN: 978-1-6150-7016-9 (sc)

Library of Congress Control Number: 2009930139

Unless otherwise noted, all Scripture quotations are taken from the Holman Christian Standard Bible (R), Copyright (C) 1999, 2000, 2002, 2003 by Holman Bible Publishers. Used by permission.

Printed in the United States of America
Bloomington, Indiana

This book is printed on acid-free paper.

To my best friend and sweetheart of fifty-three years,
Carol Ann,
whose companionship and support
have sustained our marriage and ministry together
and whose godly example
has challenged and inspired me daily
over all these years.

Table of Contents

Foreword	ix
Introduction to Difficult Times: Encouraging Words	xiii
1. The Cynic's Assault on Faith	1
2. The Cry of Pain	11
3. When Life Goes from Bad to Worse	21
4. When Life Seems Hopeless	31
5. Born for Trouble	41
6. Songs in the Night	51
7. With Friends Like You, Who Needs Enemies?	61
8. Rescue from Despair and Discouragement	73
9. Man's Inevitable Appointment	83
10. Where in the World Is God?	93
11. After Death, What?	103
12. When God Steps Down	113
13. When Wisdom Comes	123
14. Seeing God's Hand in Everything	131
15. Longing for the Good Old Days	141
16. When a Man Sees God	151
17. The Prayer that Brings Blessing	161

Foreword

The *book* of Job may be one of the least-read books of the Bible, but the *story* of Job is well known. Christians and non-Christians alike can identify Job as a man who suffered great personal pain and loss. When we say of someone, "He has the patience of Job," our reference is clearly understood. And modern tragedies are frequently described as Job-like in nature. Thus, Job and his suffering are inextricably linked in our minds.

The longer I live, the more convinced I am that those whom God would greatly use will be allowed to know great suffering. Scripture is rife with examples. Abraham knew the loss of home and the pain of waiting a lifetime for the fulfillment of God's promise. Jacob was devastated by the death of his beloved wife, Rachel, and the loss of his favorite son. Joseph was sold into slavery, falsely accused of rape, and left to languish in a foreign prison. Moses spent years in obscurity and decades leading a contentious, faithless multitude toward a land he himself would never inhabit. David was anointed king of Israel and then was hunted like a dog by Saul before he gained his rightful throne. The apostle Paul lived his entire life with a physical ailment that caused him great suffering. And the very Son of God was "a man of suffering who knew what sickness was ... stricken, struck down by God, and afflicted" (Isa. 53:3–4).

But there is more to these examples—and to Job's story—than suffering. In fact, the book of Job is less a story of tragedy than one of triumph. The ultimate result of Job's pain was great good: his life was restored, and he received a revelation of God's true character.

The book of Job has much to say to a generation living in a day that is marked by "name it and claim it" theology and the all-too-frequent preaching of a prosperity gospel. Suffering is a reality we will never escape. In fact, Christians are told to expect it and to embrace it as a means of deeper fellowship with the Lord Jesus Christ.

It is not important that we be able to understand and explain why people suffer, but it is essential that we come to understand, through suffering, who God is and how we should respond to Him. Job never understood why he suffered, but at the end of his trial, he deeply, personally, and experientially knew who God was. His response to that knowledge was to worship God, not for what God gave, but for who He was. Job's adverse circumstances, horrible as they were, were temporary. But his love for God, refined and revealed by his testing, was permanent.

What about you? Do you know Him? The apostle Paul said that knowledge was his life's one ambition. He was willing to experience both high highs and low lows to achieve it: "I also consider everything to be a loss in view of the surpassing value of knowing Christ Jesus my Lord ... My goal is to know Him and the power of His resurrection and the fellowship of His sufferings ..." (Phil. 3:8, 10).

Jimmy Draper has written *Difficult Times, Encouraging Words* so that you may know, not the answers to all the questions about man's suffering, but the truth about God's revealed character and the depths of His great, great love. The fact that Dr. Draper has tackled such a difficult subject speaks volumes about his own heart and character. I know that his desire is that when you have finished reading his book, you will be able to say along with Job: "I had heard rumors about You, but now my eyes have seen You. Therefore I take back my words and repent in dust and ashes" (Job 42:5–6).

Suffering rightly received sharpens our vision. When we see God as He truly is, we see ourselves as we truly are.

—Ed Young

Introduction to Difficult Times: Encouraging Words

Hurricane Katrina burst into our world on August 23, 2005. When she departed on August 30, the destruction was devastating. Maximum sustained winds of 175 mph had destroyed much of the Texas Gulf Coast. Storm surges of twenty-seven feet literally destroyed much of the Mississippi coastline. In New Orleans, virtually every levee was breached. There were 1,836 fatalities confirmed, and 705 people were missing. The damage done was a staggering $81.2 billion.

When 2009 was born, we felt like we had been hit again by a hurricane of even more seismic power. Like a mother who delivers after hard labor, this century has finally produced challenges that we had never faced before. This time it was the economy of our nation and world that was being destroyed. Major financial institutions were failing. Well-known national businesses were filing for bankruptcy. Unemployment rose to over 8 percent early in the year. More than 12 million Americans were unemployed by February. Few families were spared the devastation of loss of income and the devaluing of their investments. Retirement funds were lost for retirees. Many anticipating retirement soon now had to stay working for more years, assuming they still had a job!

The war of terror continues to escalate. The enemies of the West and of our American system of government and culture claim tens of thousands of "sleeper cells" are already in our country and are ready to attack us with suicide bombers. Everything we have always believed would be strong and stable seems to be coming apart. A new panic has struck our lives, and life itself seems very frightening.

Without a doubt, we are going through difficult times. There is little that we can see in our national leaders that brings us comfort or hope. Partisan politics control the decision-making processes of state and national politics. Few seem to be able to put aside personal agendas to act in the best interest of our nation.

From the Christian arena, even the evangelical leaders who dot the TV screens and radio airwaves appear to be more interested in helping us feel good about ourselves, increasing our self-images, making us feel comfortable, and promising us prosperity rather than preaching the Gospel. American evangelicalism has become a zoo filled with the wildest species of idiosyncratic individuality, isolated nomads with a menagerie of beliefs endeavoring to lead us with their promises and teachings.

Where can we turn in such a time? Only the word of God can bring us hope and encouragement for these days. Everyone is having a hard time. No one is exempt from the decay and disintegration around us. Even our churches, schools, and communities themselves have been invaded with violence and taking of innocent life. The very foundations of our lives are shifting from beneath us, and we must find some answers to the questions that arise in such times.

This volume is about the hope and encouragement that can be found from the experiences of another in his time of calamity—the life of Job. He wrestled with the questions we all ask: Where is God when I hurt?

Why is there pain? Why does God allow tragedies into our lives? Is there any hope in such times?

These pages will open up the clear and resounding answers from God Himself and bring encouraging words in these difficult times.

Chapter 1

The Cynic's Assault on Faith

Job 1:9

Let's look at a scene set in the heavens. God, who was presiding over a meeting of heavenly beings, was about to assign His angelic messengers specific tasks to perform, when Satan appears. God asked him, "Where have you been?"

Satan replied, "To tell You the truth, I have just been wandering around."

"Well, in all your wandering around, have you ever noticed My servant Job? He is a perfect, obedient, mature man, upright in all his ways."

"It's no wonder. Anyone could be good with all the blessings You have showered on him. If You take away everything he has, he will curse You."

"That is not true, and I will prove it to you. You may take all he has, but do not touch his body."

And Satan departed to afflict Job with great tragedy.

This scene from Job 1 repeats itself in Job 2. Satan appeared at another celestial meeting and God asks him, "Have you noticed that My servant Job has not cursed Me yet?"

Satan answered, "If You touch his body, he will curse You."

Confident of Job's commitment to Him, God released Satan to afflict Job's body but did not give him permission to take Job's life.

When God complimented Job for his goodness, Satan's immediate response was cynical. He declared that nobody is good without cause—nobody loves God just for the sake of loving God. Satan said in effect, "Everyone is selfish. Men only love God because God is blessing them. Job loves God because of what God has given to him, not because of who God is."

Satan's accusation was the cynic's assault on a faithful man and indeed on God Himself. Satan did not believe that Job was what God said he was: a man who served God without demanding anything in return. Satan questioned whether Job worshiped God because of the magnificence of His character or because of what God gave to him and did for him.

God is sovereign over all the earth. Yet He is not so independent that He does not care what men think of Him. He governs the earth, but He is not so arbitrary that He does not allow us freedom. According to His own self-limitation, God gives us freedom of choice. So He rejoices when a man like Job freely loves Him with all his heart. What delight God has when we love Him just because of who He is!

Satan, the opposite of Job, is the epitome of evil. His aimlessness, alienation, and anxiety drive him to oppress the souls of men. His cynicism is the natural result of his inner character. He does not know anything about the intrinsic value of righteousness that springs from an obedient heart and genuine love. To Satan, it seems that no one does anything just because it is right. No one loves God just because He is God. Every human act is prompted by a selfish ulterior motive. Everybody is looking out for number one.

And so Satan asks, "Does Job fear God for nothing?" (Job 1:9). That is the real question of the book of Job. We are accustomed to think that the question the book of Job answers is, "Why do righteous people suffer?" But the reasons for pain, suffering, injustice, and tragedy are dealt with only indirectly. The real question is the one posed in Job 1:9.

Why does man worship God? Why do prayers of faith come from both the shacks of the poor and the mansions of the rich? Why do songs of praise rise from every segment of the population? Do we worship God because we think we can get from Him what we cannot get from someone else? Do we worship Him because we think He will do for us what no one else will do for us? Do we love God because of what He gives us, or do we love God because He is God? These are questions we must consider.

Much of twentieth-century religious literature gives the impression that religion is a one-way road to health, prosperity, peace of mind, success, freedom from inhibitions, and a well-integrated personality. Many times these blessings are given, but the desire for them does not bring us to God. We do not come to God, *if we come in the proper way*, just to seek blessings from the hand of God. We come to seek the face of God. We do not worship Him for what He can do for us but for who He is. He is not some kind of cosmic genie. He is God.

Why do individuals worship God? That question is the real concern of the book of Job, and the answer lies in God Himself. If we think that answer is inadequate, then the book of Job has nothing to say to us. But those who know God declare that He is better by far than anything the world can give. Indeed, God Himself is greater than any good thing He could put into our lives.

In the book of Job we do not find logically arranged propositions that satisfy our inquiry into why people worship God. What we find is an account of Job's encounter with God. In order to find answers as we follow Job's experiences, we need to consider (1) the accuser of Job, (2) the accusation against Job, and (3) the affirmation of Job.

The Accuser

The accuser is Satan, our adversary. Clearly a malignant spirit, he questioned Job's motives. Although Job was upright in his attitude and actions toward God, Satan accused him of not worshiping God for the right reasons. Satan, who is not all-powerful or all-knowing, did not know Job's heart attitude. He was simply making accusations.

All of us need to reflect on the way we draw conclusions about other people's motives. Who are we to decide that a man's motives are different from what he says they are? We cannot see inside his heart. Any time we find ourselves criticizing someone else's motives, we should realize that we are in an area where we do not belong. That area belongs only to God. It is none of our business.

Notice that in the account of Job, Satan is not presented as a tempter. Satan did not find any weakness that would make godly Job vulnerable to temptation. So the adversary did not come to suggest evil to him; he came to accuse him.

Satan likes to play both roles: tempter and accuser. Sometimes he cannot tempt us, but he can always accuse us. That is why he is called "the accuser of our brothers" (Rev. 12:10). Satan accuses us before God and in our own hearts as well. He accuses God's children of being less than we ought to be, of being hypocritical and deceitful. He raises doubt and confusion in our minds. And so Satan made insinuations about Job.

When Satan questioned Job's motives and tried to make a deal with God, God did not accept Satan's terms. Satan twice asked God for liberty to take everything Job had, even his life. God granted Satan liberty with limitations. God is *not* the perpetrator of evil, but He permits terrible things to happen. When we suffer adversity, we frequently ask, "Why did God do that?" The answer quite simply is that God did not do it. He may *permit* something evil to happen to us, but He never *makes* evil happen to us. In fact, He draws boundaries beyond which evil cannot go.

The world is not as bad as it could be. Now the Holy Spirit restrains evil, but one day evil will be unrestrained and conditions will be much worse. During the tribulation period, the Holy Spirit will be gone from this world and evil will be permitted to run its course. If you think the world is bad now, just wait until there is no restraint!

The book of Job clearly shows that God is not the author or doer of evil. But to preserve human choice, God permits evil, within limits, until the day of the Lord when He will return and set up His Kingdom on this earth. God sets the boundaries of evil so that we may have freedom to choose how to respond to our circumstances. God in His sovereignty has decreed that we are to have liberty. We have liberty to sin and bring the consequences of sin upon ourselves and others, just as we have liberty to do what is right. God chose to give us freedom, taking the risk that our decisions may be wrong. Up to a certain limit, God allows adversity to come to us to draw out our response and reveal our attitude toward Him.

The Accusation

In many circumstances, a question can be more incisive than a declaration. This is true of the question found in Job 1:9: "Does Job fear God for nothing?" Satan was accusing Job—and all humanity—of serving God only because of the blessings God gives. Satan was claiming that no one obeys, worships, and loves God just because it is right. The adversary was insinuating that some ulterior aim or selfish motive is always involved in our worship. This accusation implies that even placing our faith in Christ is nothing more than a selfish device to escape from pain and to enjoy happiness eternally.

It is doubtful that any of us is as perfect and upright as Job was; Job is a prototype of the godly man. If his motives were ulterior, how impure must our motives be! So Satan's question was crucial, and proving him wrong was well worth Job's suffering.

Satan's accusation was not only directed toward mankind. The arrow the adversary fired did not stop until it struck God Himself. Satan was insinuating that God could no longer inspire anything but mercenary love. If Satan's premise were correct, no one would serve God because He is God, and no one would adore and worship Him simply for who He is. If Satan were correct, God would be robbed of His high and noble attributes and heaven would be robbed of its glory. Satan's accusation was against God.

Note two of the personal pronouns that appear in Job 1:11: "Stretch out *Your* hand and strike everything he owns, and he will surely curse *You* to *Your* face!" (italics added). The three Hebrew words translated "You" and "Your" here are used to address someone of equal or inferior social status. In other words, Satan in his accusation was exalting himself, making himself equal with God, and perhaps in his arrogance and pride even looking down on God.

The Affirmation

Tragedy struck; Satan took everything away from Job. Some people believe that physical possessions—houses, food, clothes, money—are the most important things in life. Job lost all his possessions. Other people say that love is the most important. Job lost that too. His children died, his wife deserted him (at least emotionally), and most of his friends forsook him. Even the special friends who came to comfort him ended up tormenting him. Job also lost his good health, which is the most important thing in life to many.

As his staggering losses piled up, Job almost lost his faith. Depressed and discouraged, he wished he could die. He asked how a man could ever be reconciled with the inequities of life. Then in chapter 38 God answered him. Out of a whirlwind the voice of God spoke and told Job that even if he had lost his hold on God, God had not lost His hold on Job.

There was tragedy in the life of Job, but there was also triumph. Job's life was the triumphant answer to Satan's accusation. Job did not serve God only because of what God did for him. Job did not worship God because He always gave him what he desired. This upright man was willing to lose family, friends, and even his life in order to prove the integrity of his faith. He declared, "Even if He kills me, I will hope in Him" (Job 13:15). This is the affirmation of Job.

Job did not barter with God for wages. He worshiped and served God without expecting reward. His longing after God's presence survived the darkness of sorrow and adversity and reached up through the darkness to lay hold of the love and light that is beyond. He possessed heart loyalty. When God Himself comes to live within a person's heart, a change takes place. Salvation does not put a person into heaven; it puts heaven into a person.

Scripture teaches that each person has the freedom to give his or her heart in faith to God. According to this theological truth, each individual has the responsibility to choose whether to repent and turn from his or her wicked ways. Another theological truth found in God's word is the sovereignty of God. According to this teaching, God controls and guides everything in the universe. Are these two truths contradictory?

We cannot reconcile these two truths with our finite minds, but both the sovereignty of God and the responsibility of man are correct doctrines. We must wait for understanding until we see Him face to face and know as we are known (1 Cor. 13:12). In the meantime, what should we do? As sincere disciples we should endeavor to find out what God wants us to do and obey Him. We should try to get in line with God's will and commit ourselves to it. We should work in harmony with what we understand to be God's purpose for our lives. When God's spirit speaks to our hearts and we respond to Him, we see the sovereignty of God and the responsibility of man working together.

The Bible may also seem contradictory regarding prosperity and persecution. Some verses seem to say, "If you serve God, obey God, and love God, you will be blessed with prosperity, health, and success." Other verses seem to say, "If you serve God, obey God, and love God, you will suffer persecution." In fact, Jesus said, "If the world hates you, understand that it hated Me before it hated you. ... If they persecuted Me, they will also persecute you" (John 15: 18, 20).

Will God make us prosperous if we serve Him? Or will God make us poor? Will He give us success? Or will we have persecution? The answer is that sometimes God gives prosperity. Sometimes God gives health. Sometimes God gives success. Sometimes God allows illness. Sometimes God allows failures. It is not ours to choose which scenario we will face. We need to accept both the pleasant and the unpleasant. Through Job, God is telling us to pursue Him no matter what the consequences may be.

We must not try to bargain with God. We must not tell God that we will do what He wants *if* He will make us successful or *if* He will heal us. The most radiant person is the one who applies the practical rule of forgetting about the consequences of following God. The most joyful person is the one who ceases to think about whether obedience will bring happiness. Such a person does what is right just because it is right, not because God is going to do something for him or her in return. We must bow before God just because He is God, not because He opens His purse and pours out riches.

We need to be brave and true and let the rewards take care of themselves. We need to act with integrity not because it helps us in business but because it is right to be honest. As children of God, we need to stand up and say, "I am going to do what God says. I will do it, not because it makes me feel good, but because it is the right thing to do."

A husband may not feel like loving his wife. He may not have the same feelings for her that he had before. The magic may be gone. What should he do? He should love her, not because he feels like loving her or because she appreciates his love, but because loving her is the right thing to do. After all, she may not appreciate his love. But her lack of appreciation does not relieve him of the responsibility of doing what is right. Someone else may make him feel good, but he must not act on the basis of his feelings.

Wives who have lost their feelings for their husbands should not act on the basis of their feelings. Neither should teenagers who don't feel like obeying their parents. The secular world tells us that we should do what makes us feel good, but God's word tells us to do the right thing no matter how we feel.

Satan's cynical question is crucial. Do we serve God because He is God or because of the blessings He gives? God is looking for people who will do what is right not because of the reward, but because it is right. He desires people who will stand not because it is always comfortable to do so but because it is right. God is gathering to Himself people who will bow before Him and put their lives at His disposal not because they always feel spiritual, but because He is God.

In answer to the cynic's assault on faith, Job said, "The Lord gives, and the Lord takes away. Praise the name of the Lord" (Job 1:21). He worshiped and served God for who He is, not for what He does.

Chapter 2

The Cry of Pain

Job 1:20–22

Pain is one thing everybody in the world has in common. In every land, in every culture, in every age, all humans cry out in pain. We cannot choose whether we will face disappointment, hurt, discouragement, sorrow, and grief. At one time or another, all of us will experience pain. We all reach out for relief in the midst of dark days and try to sort out the meaning of pain.

People cry out in pain every day. Slumping into a chair, a husband cries out, "My wife has left me. My heart is broken. What can I do?"

With trembling lips and tear-stained eyes, a wife cries out, "My husband is gone. He says he doesn't love me anymore."

A self-sufficient businessman goes to work one morning and is told that his job has been eliminated. He cries out, "How am I going to support my family?"

The parents of an unmarried teenage daughter hear the dreaded words, "Mom, Dad, I'm pregnant."

The telephone rings, and the voice at the other end of the line says, "Your son was killed in a tragic auto accident."

A mother of young children hears her physician say, "I'm sorry, but the tumor is malignant. You have cancer."

How much pain have we seen in recent months with the financial crisis of our nation? Formerly stalwart and solid business giants have been reduced to bankruptcy. Retirement funds for retirees have evaporated, and those working toward retirement must now reassess the need to keep on working beyond the time they had planned. There are battles against terrorism and a culture that is hostile to Christian faith. These and many other things have made this a painful time in which to live.

Pain is our lot in life. We cannot choose to avoid it—but we can choose *how* to face it, *how* to respond to it. What is our response to pain? Do we cry out in anger? Do we cry out in bewilderment? Do we cry out in bitterness? How do we react when we do not achieve what we set out to achieve? How do we respond when we cannot reach what we stretch to touch? What is our response when what we cherish is suddenly gone? What was Job's response when he experienced pain?

Agony

In Job 1:20–22 we see the agony Job expressed when he received news that a series of dreadful calamities had befallen him and his family. Verse 20 says, "Then Job arose, tore his robe, and shaved his head; and he fell to the ground and worshiped."

In ancient times every man of standing wore a robe over his tunic. Upon receiving tragic news, he customarily ripped that robe off as an immediate gesture of grief. Shaving the head was another ancient custom observed from Mesopotamia to Canaan. This custom was not a Hebrew tradition or a biblical injunction but a cultural way of expressing agony at a desperate time.

As the blows fell on Job, he felt his losses. He experienced grief. He felt the agony of bereavement and disappointment. He experienced all the emotions we experience during painful times.

Many people today tell us, "If you feel grief, something is wrong with you." They make us feel guilty when we express our grief. They say, "You are to be above that. Only weak people grieve." How wrong they are! They miss the clear teaching of the word of God. If we do not grieve when tragedy comes, we become less like God.

We know that God experiences grief, for Ephesians 4:30 says, "Don't grieve God's Holy Spirit, who has sealed you for the day of redemption." God grieves over our sin because He loves us. Although God is not the author or practitioner of sin, He understands sin and its impact on us. Grief arises from the emotion of love, and God is love (1 John 4:8, 16). God loves us, and He understands our grief.

Grief is an appropriate emotion, a normal and natural response to the pain we feel. Instead of being a sign of weakness, grief demonstrates love and concern. Grief is not sin. It is not wrong to feel pain, and it is not wrong to feel grief when we experience pain. We are not surprised when a person with a broken arm hurts and expresses pain, and we can expect a person with a broken heart to hurt and to express the pain he feels. That kind of agony is very real and important. There is no sin in mourning over the loss of someone or something we love. Job lost everything, and he expressed the agony he felt.

There is a difference, though, between how believers grieve and how unbelievers grieve. The apostle Paul said, "We do not want you to be uninformed, brothers, concerning those who are asleep, so that you will not grieve like the rest, who have no hope" (1 Thess. 4:13). People whose lives are not grounded in Jesus Christ grieve out of despair and hopelessness. God's children who experience the loss of loved ones do not grieve hopelessly. That is the difference God makes in our lives.

Adoration

After Job expressed his agony, he "fell to the ground and worshiped" (Job 1:20). He fell not in despair or bitterness or anger, but in submission to and adoration of God. As his face touched the ground, his body revealed the attitude of his heart. When grief pressed Job to the ground, he turned the ground into a shrine and worshiped there.

When tragedy strikes us, we can turn our circumstances into a shrine and worship God in them. We can make a shrine in the depths of our darkness and worship God there. We can fall on our faces in submission and adoration. We can adore Him wherever we are and in whatever emotional state we find ourselves. That is the lesson we learn from Job in this scene.

When our hearts are pressed down, we can cry out to God in our pain and He will hear us. When disappointments, pain, and grief are real, He is there. Our greatest opportunities for worship and praise come when pain forces us to our knees and we fall prostrate before God.

Acknowledgment

After Job expressed adoration, he acknowledged his dependence upon God. His statement in Job 1:21 is one of the most meaningful expressions found anywhere in literature. Spoken from the depths of a broken heart, it reveals one man's ready acceptance of the will of God. Job said:

> Naked I came from my mother's womb,
> And naked I will leave this life.
> The Lord gives, and the Lord takes away;
> Praise the name of the Lord.

Job recognized that he had come into the world with nothing and he would leave it with nothing. In his brief but profound declaration, Job acknowledged a spectacular truth about life. He declared that it is possible for a man to be stripped of everything life has given him and still lack nothing. Even if everything we believe to be meaningful in life is taken away, we will still have all we need for eternity. We will take nothing out of this life except what we have become in our relationship with God. "Only one life, 'twill soon be past; Only what's done for Christ will last."

Notice how Job described life: "I came ... I [shall] return." Coming and returning is what life is all about. In the intervening years we tend to give ourselves to attaining things we cannot keep and focus our attention on things that are absolutely irrelevant to the real meaning of life.

Since people in every culture try to find the meaning of the process of coming and returning, there are many different philosophies of life. Communism with its dialectic materialism, capitalism with its emphasis on free enterprise, socialism with its shared poverty, and humanism with its arrogant self-sufficiency all try to provide some purpose for life in the present. Religions with contrived deities try to explain the purpose of the coming and returning experience. But the true meaning of life can be found only in the biblical revelation of God, the great Creator who became our Savior. When we are related to Him through faith, we can find meaning in the process of coming and returning. All that we have, all that we are, and all that we can ever hope to be is wrapped up in the person of the Lord.

Acclamation

Job's acknowledgment included acclamation of the Lord. He recognized God's sovereign right to do whatever He pleased. Job did not demand his own rights. He did not say, "I have a right to be happy. I have a right to a good living. I have a right to a good family." His perspective was God-centered, not self-centered.

Job's initial response to his calamities was not a display of anger. It did not even occur to Job then to be angry with those desert raiders who stole his livestock and killed his servants. It did not occur to Job to be angry with the frontier guards whose carelessness allowed the raiders to cross the border. It did not occur to Job to be angry with his servants who timidly stood by and watched the raids. It did not occur to Job to be angry with the weather—or the God of the weather—when a windstorm killed his children. In everything that happened, Job saw the hand of a sovereign God. He acknowledged God's sovereignty and worshiped Him on the spot. Job worshiped God for who He was, not for what He had given to him.

God did not cause these natural disasters, and He was not defeated by them. Neither is God defeated by the cancer that racks our bodies, the loneliness that rends our hearts, or the pain that pierces our flesh. God is not defeated by the despair that shatters our minds, the discouragement that shrouds our beings, or the disappointment that invades our experiences. God is bigger than all these things.

Job understood that God was not too small for his circumstances. God was not defeated by them, nor was He lost in their wake. In the midst of Job's darkness and despair, God was still there. Job's attitude was similar to that of the apostle Paul, who wrote:

> Who can separate us from the love of Christ? Can affliction or anguish or persecution or famine or nakedness of danger or sword? … No, in all these things we are more than victorious through Him who loved us. For I am persuaded that neither death nor life, nor angels nor rulers, nor things present, nor things to come, nor powers, nor height, nor depth, nor any other created thing, will have the power to separate us from the love of God that is in Christ Jesus our Lord! (Rom. 8:35–39)

No wonder Job cried out, "Praise the name of the Lord!" (Job 1:21)

We need to be like Job and see the hand of God in everything. Job looked on all he possessed as gifts from God: cattle, flocks, herds, servants, land, and even family. Because he did not attribute his success and wealth to any source other than God, he did not become bitter or resentful when he lost everything. We need to learn the wisdom of never attributing our comfort, pleasure, or prosperity to any earthly source. Whatever good we enjoy in this life is God's doing, not ours. How sweet it is to realize that everything in life is a gift from God. All our gains are placed into our hands by Him.

The gifts we receive from God are undeserved. God gives us gifts because He chooses to give us gifts, not because we deserve them. Understanding this truth will give us a proper perspective on our possessions. We will not feel proud if we have more than someone else, and we will not become bitter if we have less.

We are stewards of whatever gracious gifts God chooses to give us. We are to watch over them, but they belong to Him alone. Just as we belong to Him, His gifts to us belong to Him. They are His, and He can do whatever He pleases with them. Being only stewards, we know that He may choose to take His gifts away. Whether He gives or takes, "Praise the name of the Lord."

When we grasp the truth that everything belongs to God and we have been placed in charge of His belongings, we experience more joy in giving them back to God. It is a joy to acknowledge Him with all we have and all we do. It is our privilege to use what God has given to us in service for Him.

Job did not serve God because of what He gave him, and Job did not worship the gifts God gave; he worshiped the Lord who gave the gifts. We too should worship the Lord, not His gifts. We degrade ourselves when we worship the gifts, but we do it so often. A wife may worship her husband who is God's gift to her. A husband may worship a wife. Parents may worship their children. Children may worship their parents. We may worship our businesses or our successes.

We all have the potential to worship the gifts of God instead of God the giver. When the gifts of God occupy the place of priority in our lives, we fall into a form of idolatry. We must never let secondary things occupy a place of primary significance in our lives. Only the Lord belongs on the throne of our hearts. "The Lord gives ... Praise the name of the Lord." Worship God alone. Praise Him!

During times of prosperity we are more prone to sin than during times of adversity. That is a trait of the human condition. Rarely is a person prompted to get right with God when he is experiencing success and has money in the bank. Success and riches tend to turn our hearts away from God. We begin to focus on the gifts rather than the giver. Often we turn back to God only when our lives fall apart and the foundation we have built collapses. In times of prosperity we need to realize the truth of this hymn:

> Prone to wander, Lord, I feel it,
> Prone to leave the God I love;
> Here's my heart, O take and seal it;
> Seal it for Thy courts above.[1]

We need to be grateful during times of prosperity. God blesses us every day with life, breath, and health. We have much more than we deserve, and we need to be thankful. Learning to be appreciative in good times will help us learn to praise God in bad times.

It is easy to praise the Lord when good news comes along, but when tragedy comes, it is hard. Job was able to praise the Lord in bad times because he had practiced being appreciative in good times. He had learned to say, "Praise God from whom all blessings flow." He had learned to acknowledge that everything he had came from God and belonged to Him. So when calamity befell him, it was quite appropriate and natural for Job to be grateful to God. In times of prosperity or adversity, Job could say, "The Lord gives, and the Lord takes away; Praise the name of the Lord."

In times of trouble Satan tells us to curse God. That is what he tried to get Job to do (Job 1:11), but Job refused. Job demonstrated a good rule to follow: do the opposite of whatever Satan tells you to do! That rule is the key to defeating Satan. If we are tempted to do the wrong thing, we should do the right thing. If Satan urges us to curse God, we should bless Him. If we do the opposite of what Satan encourages us to do, God will bless us and He will be honored. Our lives will say, "Praise the name of the Lord."

The Lord dwells in the praises of His people. If we are middle-aged skeptics who have been through hard times, we should praise the name of the Lord. When our bodies are racked with pain and the future is clouded with uncertainty, we should praise the name of the Lord. If we have the innocence, buoyancy, and excitement of a child, we should praise the name of the Lord. Whatever our circumstances are, we should be able to see the hand of God and say, "Praise the name of the Lord."

Appreciation

Job's acclamation was full of appreciation. "Throughout all this Job did not sin or blame God for anything" (Job 1:22). If we were placed in his situation, how many of us would react as Job did? How many of us would respond to adversity with adoration? How many would maintain moral integrity? How many would not bend to bitterness? How many of us would refuse to blame God?

Job refused to blame God for his misfortunes, and his amazing response shows us that it is possible for devotion to come from the heart without regard for a reward. It is possible for man to be godly apart from hope for material gain. It is possible for an individual to walk with God even when God does not remove the pain or hurt from life's experiences.

Job's heart was focused on God. In all his ways he acknowledged Him. When tragedy came, it was not hard for Job to praise the Lord because his worship of God was not just a side effect of his prosperity. He worshiped God regardless of his circumstances. He praised God in prosperity and in pain.

Job 1 begins with God praising Job for his uprightness and Job being blessed with material comfort and a wonderful family. The chapter continues with Job enduring tragedies and ends with Job continuing to bless the name of our sovereign God. Job 1 is a preview of the entire book of Job. The conclusion in Job 42 is the same as the conclusion of Job 1. All the chapters between Job 1 and Job 42 build up to that repeated conclusion.

The entire book of Job provides help as we endeavor to respond to our own pain. We will all cry out in pain sometime in our lives. We will all find our lives shrouded in darkness at one time or another. We will all reach out in despair. Corporately and individually we will all experience suffering; that fact is as certain as life itself. The only uncertainty is *how* we will cry out. Will we cry out in anger and bitterness, or will we cry out in faith and trust? May our response to pain be based on faith in God! May we trust in spite of our pain. May we acknowledge from our hearts that everything we are or ever hope to be is wrapped up in our Lord. May we respond as Job did.

Endnotes

1 From "Come Thou Fount of Every Blessing" by Robert Robinson.

Chapter 3

When Life Goes from Bad to Worse

Job 3:25–26

During World War II a seaman was unable to return from leave on time. He wrote the following letter of explanation to the executive officer of his warship:

I received ten days' leave to visit my brother who lives on a farm in Arkansas. On September 11 my brother's barn burned down, all except the brick silo, the top of which was damaged by a bolt of lightning, which started the fire.

On September 12 my brother decided to repair the silo. To help him I rigged a barrel hoist to the top of the silo so that bricks could be hoisted to a platform we had erected up there.

After the work was done, there were a lot of bricks left over. I filled the barrel, then climbed down the ladder and untied the line to let the barrel down. However, the barrel was heavier than I was and when it started down, I started up.

By the time I thought of letting go, I was so far up that it was safer to hang on. Halfway up, the barrel hit me on the shoulder pretty hard but I hung on, as my division officer told me always to do when holding a line. I was going pretty fast at the top, and bumped my head hard.

When the barrel hit the ground the bottom fell out of it, letting all the bricks out. I was then heavier than the barrel and started down again. As the barrel passed me it hit me on the other shoulder. I must have landed pretty hard on the pile of bricks because I lost my presence of mind and let go of the line, upon which the barrel came down pretty fast and hit me on top of the head.

The doctor wouldn't let me start back to the ship until September 17, which made me two days over leave, which I don't think is too much under the circumstances.[1]

Have you ever had a day like the seaman had on that September 12? We all have in recent days. Our world has been turned upside down by terrorism, failing financial structures, unemployment, political chaos and irresponsibility, and many other things. There are days when life goes from bad to worse. Things start out bad and go downhill. If we don't discover an attitude or philosophy that enables us to deal with days like that, we won't survive. The book of Job tells us what to do when things go from bad to worse.

What Happened to Job?

Job 1:13–19 tells us all that happened to Job on one bad day. He lost all his possessions—all his property, animals, and servants. This loss would be the equivalent of your house burning down and your business going bankrupt on the same day. One day he was wealthy and self-sufficient, and the next day he had nothing. Many of us have suffered the loss of things we had counted on and our hopes have been dashed; we can identify with Job.

Job also lost his children. Tornado-like winds swept across the plain and in one fell swoop destroyed his son's house and killed all his children. Some of us have lost children through death. Some of us have lost children through rebellion; they are alive, but we do not have anger-free fellowship with them. We can identify with Job's loss.

Soon after the first tragic day, Job lost his health. He was stricken with "incurable boils from the sole of his foot to the top of his head" (Job 2:7). He could not stand without standing on a boil. He could not sit without sitting on a boil. He could not lie down without lying on a boil. Some of us can identify with Job's loss of health. Heart attacks, cancer, high blood pressure, and other diseases have caused our physical stamina to deteriorate. Our strength and vigor is gone.

Then Job lost harmony in his home. Instead of encouraging her sick husband, Job's wife said to him, "Do you still retain your integrity? Curse God and die!" (Job 2:9). Perhaps you can identify with this loss of harmony and support. Perhaps you and your spouse once lived together happily but now experience tension, isolation, and barriers.

Job lost his reputation too. He had been thought of as a great, honest, and God-fearing man, but when people heard about his calamities, they concluded that he was hiding something sinful. Those of us who have been slandered can certainly identify with Job. When a person loses the good reputation he has worked so hard to build, he suffers pain.

When Job's friends who came to grieve with him saw him, they tore their robes, sprinkled dust on their heads, and wept. They appeared to be supportive friends, but as soon as they began to speak, their hostility became evident. They were antagonists, not friends. If you have ever lost a friend or a friend has misrepresented you, if someone you really care about has become estranged, you can identify with Job. In addition to all his other losses, Job lost his friends. Life was going from bad to worse.

What Did Job Do?

Job did seven things when his situation worsened. No matter how bad the circumstances, the events, the emotions, the tragedy, or the situation may be, we can follow these same positive steps today.

1. *He worshiped God and renewed his commitment to Him.* "Then Job stood up, tore his robe and shaved his head. He fell to the ground and worshiped" (Job 1:20). Shaving one's head and tearing one's robe were acts of humility, of confession, of laying oneself before God. The first thing Job did when things went from bad to worse was to get on his knees to praise and worship God. Normally our first reaction is to get angry and blame someone. In our frustration as we look for some way to relieve the tension, we may strike out at others. Job, however, bowed before God and worshiped Him.

2. *He declared his faith in God.* After a day of tragic losses, Job declared that the Lord was the giver of blessings and He had the right to take blessings away. Then he praised the name of the Lord (Job 1:21). Job understood, as we need to understand, that God owes us nothing. Any good thing we receive is a gift of grace: what we desperately need, but have no right to ask for, is given simply because God loves us. Because Job understood the grace of God, he was able to declare his trust in God even though his circumstances were desperate. Many of our troubles would fade into insignificance if we would start praising God.

3. *He did not accuse God.* "Throughout all this Job did not sin or blame God for anything" (Job 1:22). When his wife encouraged him to curse God and die, he rebuked her: "'You speak as a foolish woman speaks,' he told her. 'Should we accept only good from God and not adversity?' Throughout all this Job did not sin in what he said" (Job 2:10). Job did not accuse God of making a mistake.

As a pastor I frequently had to counsel a family after a tragedy happened. Invariably someone in the family asked the question, "Why did God do this? Why did God let his happen?" My answer was, "Do not blame God."

God does not sit around thinking of ways to hurt us. We must not blame God for our troubles. We may not understand why things happen as they do—the same sun that scorches one flower gives life to another—but we must not accuse God. Our anger over the turmoil in our lives is an accusation against God, but we cannot gain spiritual victory when we are hostile to God.

4. He declared his confidence in the purposes of God. Job said, "I know You can do anything and no plan of Yours can be thwarted" (Job 42:2). We serve a God who is not upset by the things that happen. His plans cannot be derailed. His purposes will be accomplished. God is going to work out that which is best for us and that which gives glory to Him.

5. He confessed that he did not understand everything. Job confessed to God: "You asked, 'Who is this who conceals My counsel with ignorance?' Surely I spoke about things I did not understand, things too wonderful for me to know" (Job 42:3). Job admitted that he talked a lot but really did not understand what he was talking about; he admitted he had an inadequate perspective, that he did not understand everything. How refreshing his honesty is! We are prone to make judgments and pronouncements, so it is important for us to realize that our understanding is limited and so is our perspective. Only God knows everything. That is why we can and should trust Him.

6. He turned his heart toward God. Job said to God: "You said, 'Listen now, and I will speak. When I question you, you will inform Me.' I had heard rumors about You, but now my eyes have seen You" (Job 42:4–5). Job declared that he personally encountered God during his trials. If we turn our hearts toward God during our trials, we too will find Him. In every experience, in every circumstance, let us lift our hearts to the Lord. He is there when we seek Him from the midst of difficulties.

7. He turned himself toward God in repentance. Job saw his unworthiness and repented of it. "Therefore I take back my words and repent in dust and ashes" (Job 42:6). Repentance toward God opens the door for Him to move in great power and blessing in our lives.

What We Can Learn

We can learn five lessons from what Job experienced.

1. *Any religious experience that causes us to feel superior to others is artificial and hypocritical.* The person who declares that he or she is spiritual is not! Job's three friends came with "a word from God." They said in effect, "These calamities have come upon you because you are wicked. You are suffering because you are not right with God." They spoke from a presumed position of superior spirituality, but scripture reveals their true status. God said to Eliphaz, "I am angry with you and your two friends, for you have not spoken the truth about Me, as My servant Job has" (Job 42:7).

Job himself started out maintaining how righteous he was. He argued that he was not a sinner. By the end of the book, however, he was saying in effect, "I am nothing but dirt. I hate what I see in myself." Then he repented and came to God.

The closer we get to God, the more we realize that the only good in us is Jesus. We are not good in ourselves. We are saved by grace, and we serve by grace. We have feet of clay and hearts that are prone to disobey God. Only when the Holy Spirit fills us and controls us is He able to lead us and reveal Himself through us.

Many of us have become so sophisticated that we do not want to admit that there might be spiritual needs in our lives. But the best Christians seem to be the first to confess their need of the Savior. I learned when I was a boy that the people who are the most genuinely spiritual are the ones who are most keenly aware of their inadequacies. They are not arrogant. They understand that nothing good dwells in them (Rom. 7:18). In our flesh—in our strength—there is nothing valuable. God alone can make something worthwhile out of us.

2. *God's purpose does not always result in human success.* Some people may say, "Job got his family back," but they are wrong. He got another

family. He still grieved over the loss of his sons, daughters, and servants and over the breach in fellowship with his wife.

Jeremiah, the Old Testament prophet most like Jesus, was a failure by human standards of success. This tenderhearted man, known as "the weeping prophet," was rejected by his family, his neighborhood, his city, his nation, and his king. Ultimately Jeremiah was taken away as a captive, and he died in Egypt. Yet he fulfilled God's purpose for his life.

In the New Testament, Stephen was stoned to death. God's purpose for Stephen clearly did not result in human success, but He used this first Christian martyr to thrust the Christian movement into the area of conflict.

John the Baptist was another man who had an inglorious death. His head was put on a platter and presented to a pagan king. Human success was not God's purpose for him.

A few years ago United Press International released the story of a twelve-year-old boy who was summarily executed by a Soviet-trained Afghan prison commander. Because the boy believed in God, he was held for two weeks in the dark cells of a secret-police headquarters and tortured with electric shocks and beatings. Then he was taken to prison. The first night he was there, the prison commander found him praying in his crowded cell.

"So you are praying to your God," the commander said.

"Yes, I always pray. Don't you?" replied the boy.

"If your God exists, ask Him to release you. I can kill you, and your God cannot save you. You see, there is no God," answered the commander.

Very quietly the boys said, "You are a bad man. You do not believe in God."

In response, the commander killed the boy. That scene is hardly a picture of success from the world's standpoint.

God's purpose does not always result in human success. We cannot find the "prosperity gospel" in the book of Job. The most damaging heresy in the world today is that which states that faithfulness to God always results in human success.

3. *God does not condemn our doubts and questions.* In the end God praised Job, who had all the questions, and condemned his three friends, who thought they had all the answers. In the pit of despair Job had some terrible thoughts and questions: "I hate the day I was born. Why didn't I die at birth? Why is my birthday even remembered? I wish I had never been born." His questions rolled like a torrent, but God did not condemn Job because he had questions. God can handle our honest doubts and questions. We need only bring them to Him.

There was truth in what Job's three friends said, but not the whole truth. For example, what one of his friends said in Job 5:17 is true: "Do not reject the discipline of the Almighty." But Job's friends were playing with the truth. They believed only what they wanted to believe and drew conclusions that were false. So God rejected Job's friends. But he accepted Job because his doubts and questions were honest.

Today some people preach part of the truth as if it were the whole truth. The acceptance of partial truth is one of the greatest dangers we face; it is the cause of most of the confusion in the Christian world.

4. *Fulfillment is found not in our understanding, but in our obedience.* We do not have to understand everything. God never did answer Job's questions, but by the end of the book, Job no longer had any questions! Which is best: to have all our questions answered or to have all our questions removed? Job had such deep satisfaction in his new experience with God that the questions did not matter anymore. He simply trusted God and found fulfillment in Him.

5. *Victory is found when we pray for those who accuse us.* One of the most profound lessons in the Bible is revealed in God's words to Eliphaz: "I am angry with you and your two friends, for you have not spoken the truth about Me, as My servant Job has. Now take seven bulls and seven rams, go to My servant Job, and offer a burnt offering for yourselves. Then My servant Job will pray for you" (Job 42:7–8). These men had

assaulted Job. They had told him that he was not spiritual and that he needed to repent and get right with God. They had accused him and been belligerent toward him. And God instructed them to go to Job so that Job could pray for them!

What happened to Job when he prayed for his antagonists? "After Job had prayed for his friends, the Lord restored his prosperity and doubled his previous possessions" (Job 42:10).

When things go from bad to worse, the final step to victory over bitterness is to pray for the one who caused the bitterness. Job had bitterness in his heart toward his friends who attacked him when he was hurting so badly from all his losses. Job must have endured the attacks for a long time, and he responded by asking God and his friends some angry questions. Then God told Job to remove the bitterness, forgive his friends, and pray for them. If we had been in Job's position, most of us would not have understood that command, nor would we have been willing to obey it.

If we do not deal with bitterness, it will grow in our hearts and destroy everything that is good in our lives. Hebrews 12:14–15 tells us, "Pursue peace with everyone, and holiness—without it no one will see the Lord. See to it that no one falls short of the grace of God and that no root of bitterness springs up, causing trouble and by it, defiling many." The phrase "springs up" is derived from a Greek word that speaks of the growth of a poisonous plant. When we allow bitterness to spring up inside us, it grows like a poisonous plant until it destroys us. So we must deal with bitterness in the way scripture teaches.

If we want victory, we must pray for those who are responsible for our anguish. If your spouse has caused bitterness in your heart, pray for him or her. If parents, friends, children, employers, or enemies have caused bitterness, pray for them. If we do not learn this secret, we will have many days when things go from bad to worse. If we learn this secret, we can stop the roller coaster of blame and hostility. There will still be experiences we do not want to face, but if we pray for those we believe are responsible and forgive them, God will remove the bitterness from our hearts and give us peace and joy.

Job's prayer for his friends signified forgiveness. Jesus said that if we forgive others their trespasses, God will forgive us (Matt. 6:14). If we do not forgive them, God will not forgive us. Jesus was declaring very plainly that if our hearts are right with God, we will have forgiving hearts. So let us follow Job's example and with forgiving hearts pray for those who accuse us.

Endnotes

1 "Tall Tale" submitted by E. A. Meola, *Reader's Digest*, January 1943, 74.

Chapter 4

When Life Seems Hopeless

Job 3:20–23

Few people have ever had more right than Job had to feel that life was hopeless. In a sudden reversal of circumstances, his prosperity, prestige, family stability, and good health were replaced by financial and personal ruin. He lost everything he owned, including his reputation. His home life was in a shambles, and he was in physical misery.

In Job 3, Job described his anguish and trouble as "darkness" surrounding him. In his distress he even wished that he had never been born. But since he had been born and there was nothing he could do about that, he wished he could die. He was in a desperate situation. He had nothing tangible to hold onto, and even his wife had turned against him. The friends who had come to comfort him were questioning his reputation, and the only recourse he had left was his faith.

Job had always been a man of faith. Faith had been the factor by which he had interpreted all of life's experiences. His faith had been central to his life before tragedy struck, so when trouble came it was natural for Job to interpret it in terms of his faith and to look to his faith for solace. But Job's faith provided no answers to his questions.

He looked up through tears and cursed his birth. He felt that life had lost its meaning, and he even feared that God had forsaken him. With bitter words he expressed the anguish, depression, and loneliness he was experiencing as a result of terrible physical pain and personal loss. Job would not curse God, but he seethed in his agony and became quite angry. We cannot blame Job for being angry.

A person of faith may become angry—and it is possible for him to express his anger in a healthy way. The believer may ask why. The skeptics and the atheists have no need to ask why tragedy comes or why pain is inflicted. Their mindset tells them that they are the victims of chance. They have convinced themselves that whatever happens, happens. In their view, pain and suffering are inevitable, merely natural occurrences of the human experience. People who refuse to believe in God have no questions. They accept misfortunes as the capricious twists of fate.

For the person who has faith in God, the problem of pain is difficult. He wonders why an all-powerful God who governs the universe permits evil. If God governs humanity, why does He permit pain and suffering? If God knows us personally, why does He permit us to have difficulties? Does He really care? It would be absolutely absurd for the children of God not to ask why. *Why?* is a question of faith. Because we believe there is a God and that He does care, we look through the eyes of faith for the answer to the problem of pain.

Job's search for answers had driven him to desperation. Some desperate moments are so bleak, painful, and dark that we come to the end of our own resources and we wish we could die. Who among us has not said, "They would be better off if I were not here"? Who has not said, "I am worth more dead than I am alive"? That is the state of mind in which Job found himself.

Before he was afflicted, Job had a complete worldview. His religion met his needs and his family's needs. Job had a very comfortable theology. He believed there was a God who, being all-powerful, guided the affairs of mankind and being all-knowing, always governed justly.

It was natural and logical for Job to conclude that God prospered the righteous and punished the wicked. Sometimes the punishment came in the form of affliction. Because of that theology Job's friends blamed his afflictions on some sin in his life. They believed that his suffering would be relieved if he confessed his sin. Today some individuals preach the same theology. It is not new.

Because of his theology, Job was perplexed when suffering and pain came to him. He felt isolated and abandoned. He was lonely and depressed. Since he could not identify any cause for his affliction, his life lost its meaning. He could not look to his children for comfort; they were dead. He could not ask his wife for help; she had turned her back on him. God—the only friend he thought he had left—seemed to have forsaken him. Still Job refused to curse God or accuse Him.

Because Job refused to curse God, he was consumed with righteous anger. Righteous anger, the hottest of passions and coldest of emotions working simultaneously, cries out in fury. So from the depths of his heart, Job cried, "Why?" Seven times in this chapter he called out, "Why?"

The entire third chapter of Job is the lament of one who was a total victim of his troubles. Job was completely disoriented by his difficulties, and he lacked understanding of what was taking place in his life. The very foundation upon which he had been standing spiritually, intellectually, and emotionally had been cut out from under him. He was discouraged, perplexed, helpless, and hopeless.

Life has become hopeless for many people in our world today. They feel that there are no answers, and they see no way out of their difficulties. With Job they say, "Why is light given to one burdened with grief, and life to those whose existence is bitter?" (Job 3:20). They wonder, "Why is life given to a man whose path is hidden, whom God has hedged in?" (Job 3:23). The word translated "hedged in" is the same word used in Job 1:10 where Satan said to God, "Haven't You placed a hedge around him, his household, and everything he owns?" Satan was talking about a protective hedge, but Job was referring to a hedge of restriction. In effect Job was asking, "What is the good of receiving light when I am so restricted that I cannot respond to it with the understanding God has given me?"

Job could see no way out of his circumstances. He felt hedged in, helpless, and hopeless. He was *not* contemplating suicide or asking for someone to kill him. He was just so miserable that he wished he were dead. Seeing no solution to the difficulties that confronted him, he simply cried out in anguish and asked God to put him out of his misery. The discourse in Job 3 reveals the extreme to which pain can drive a person. Very few of us have felt such excruciating pain that we longed for death.

Speaking of the day of his birth, Job used the words "darkness" three times and "gloom" once in Job 3:1–9. Four different Hebrew words, which are translated "darkness" or "gloom" in this passage, reveal Job's desire that information about him be shrouded in darkness so that even God could not see it. He wanted his birthday to be erased from the calendar: "May it not appear among the days of the year or be listed in the calendar" (Job 3:6).

Job asked: "Why was I not stillborn; why didn't I die when I came from the womb?" (Job 3:11). Weary with agony, he was comparing the quietness and stillness of death with the trouble and agitation of life. If he had been stillborn, he would be free from trouble and disease.

Job's heart cried out in anguish as he described his restless condition. His words were not evidence of a sick mind or a warped personality. They were the response of a healthy, searching mind confronting the inescapable fact of pain. Job did not have the diseased melancholy of an emotionally disturbed person. He simply had the courage to ask why he was suffering and how long his suffering would endure.

Such questions are legitimate when they come from people of faith. These questions are not appropriate, however, when they come from people who do not know and trust the Lord. People who do not believe there is a God who is interested in our well-being and who guides our lives cannot logically expect there to be answers to the problems of death, pain, suffering, and inequity.

As believers we know that when sin entered the world, death, pain, suffering, and inequity came with it (Gen. 3:14–24; Rom. 5:12; 8:18–23). But we also know that in the beginning God designed the world to be free from pain. Like Job, we struggle to understand why the present reality is one of pain and suffering even though God does care about us. We must ask our questions and seek the answers.

In Job 3, Job directed his questions toward God. Although he did not curse God, accuse Him, or turn his back on Him, he asked God a series of probing questions as he sought to understand his situation. Those questions are structured to direct us to God.

As Job brooded in silent misery over the tragedies that had befallen him, he knew he was in danger of losing his faith. So what did he do? He turned his heart toward God. Turning toward God is the key to solving the mysteries of life. When circumstances are beyond our control and we too feel hopeless, helpless, and perplexed, we should turn our hearts toward God. When we do, we will be following along the path blazed by Job.

God was the direction of Job's life. As he searched for answers, he reached out to God. Job involved God in his situation. Even his suggestion that God had hedged him in (Job 3:23) showed that Job's thoughts were turning toward God.

God responded to Job's questions (Job 38–40). In the midst of a storm Job heard God's voice. "Then the Lord answered Job from the whirlwind" (Job 38:1). God disclosed Himself to the one who had diligently sought Him. Just as the voice of God strengthened Job's faith, the word of God will strengthen our faith.

When we hear the voice of God in the midst of our trouble, we will experience the victory of faith. On dark days when everything seems hopeless, we should turn toward God and listen for His voice. If we listen for Him, we will hear Him. He will never turn away from us when we turn toward Him. Our Lord said, "Come to Me, all of you who are weary and burdened, and I will give you rest. All of you, take up My yoke and learn from Me, because I am gentle and humble in heart, and you will find rest for yourselves. For My yoke is easy and My burden is light" (Matt. 11:28–30).

In the midst of his turmoil Job cried out, "Even if He kills me, I will hope in Him. I will still defend my ways before Him" (Job 13:15). Job felt free to present his arguments boldly before God because he had a personal relationship with Him. Job knew that he had access to God in his time of need. Job's faith reached out and claimed the presence of God. He exclaimed, "But I know my living Redeemer, and He will stand on the dust at last. Even after my skin has been destroyed, yet I will see God in my flesh" (Job 19:25–26).

Job's faith is a lesson to us. Job did not understand the reason for his troubles, nor did he see any way out of his circumstances. Nevertheless, believing that God was somehow involved in his life and circumstances, he trustfully reached out to Him. An act of faith is the beginning of every personal relationship with God (Gen. 15:6; John 1:12; 5:24). When we have a personal relationship with Him, we can trustfully turn to God, who gives victory over our circumstances. The victory that overcomes is the victory we have in Jesus Christ. "Whatever has been born of God conquers the world. This is the victory that has conquered the world: our faith" (1 John 5:4).

Several years ago a lady came to me for counseling. She felt her husband was cold, unemotional, unloving, uncaring, and insensitive to her needs. Tired of her marital circumstances, she wanted someone to change her husband. After several conferences with her, I told her to go home, get on her knees, and tell the Lord how miserable she was. Then I told her to tell God that if He wanted her to be miserable the rest of her life, she was willing to be miserable. To say that she left my office in anger is an understatement.

Several months later the lady came back. "After I got over being angry," she said, "I did what you suggested. I got down on my knees and told the Lord I was willing to be miserable the rest of my life if that was what He wanted." Then she said, "You know, my husband has become everything I wanted him to be," and she proceeded to tell me how wonderful he was. I knew the couple well, and I knew that her husband had not changed. She had changed. She had taken a desperate situation to the Lord and had trusted Him to do what was best. She had turned to the Lord, and He had delivered her out of her misery. That couple are still married and now have grandchildren. The husband still has not changed, but God has given the wife the victory of faith.

God turns desperate, hopeless situations into glorious victories. When we turn to Him in faith, He performs His work in our circumstances and weaknesses. I cannot tell you how He delivers the victory. Only God knows how. I just know that when we hear God's voice in the whirlwind, there is victory in faith. When we do what God tells us to do and commit ourselves to His will and purpose, there is victory even in the darkest hours of our lives.

In those darkest hours, our real selves are revealed. We don't know what is really inside us until we have to respond to life's trials and tests. Sometimes our need for repentance is exposed. In the book of Job we learn about the value of repentance.

Job said, "Therefore I take back my words and repent in dust and ashes" (Job 42:6). When he finally saw God as He is and himself as he was, he repented of his self-centeredness and his misconceptions and was brought closer to God. Likewise when we use our dark moments to confess our sin and lay our lives open before God, we will be brought nearer to Him.

In our dark moments we learn that God is sufficient. The apostle Paul, who had a physical affliction, wrote: "Concerning this, I pleaded with the Lord three times to take it away from me. But He said to me,

'My grace is sufficient for you, for power is perfected in weakness'" (2 Cor. 12:8–9).

When our hearts are pressed down and the days seem hopeless, turning to God helps us realize who we are and how important we are to God. He draws us to Himself.

When we go through our valleys of suffering, we should read Hebrews 11 for encouragement. The saints in that chapter traveled our road. If we look at that road, we will see our own footprints. If we look more closely, we will see the footprints of the martyrs who went before us. If we look even more carefully, we will see the footprints of the Son of God who preceded us all. Some glorious ministries emerged from the suffering of our predecessors, and we may be privileged to see good coming from our difficulties. Hebrews 12:1–2 refers to the gallery of saints in Hebrews 11:

> Therefore since we also have such a large cloud of witnesses surrounding us, let us lay aside every weight and the sin that so easily ensnares us, and run with endurance the race that lies before us, keeping our eyes on Jesus, the source and perfecter of our faith, who for the joy that lay before Him endured a cross and despised the shame, and has sat down at the right hand of God's throne.

Many of us devote most of our lives to gaining what we don't need in order to impress people we don't like. We seldom take time to smell the roses or enjoy what we have been given. Then disappointments come and our desperate moments help us rearrange our priorities and focus on the important things in life. Suffering purifies our motives and makes us contrite. When we turn in contrition to God, we come to rest in Him by faith.

Suffering brings us into the presence of Christ and helps us get to know Him. We should share the apostle Paul's desire to "know Him and the power of His resurrection, and the fellowship of His sufferings, being conformed to His death, assuming that I will somehow reach the resurrection from among the dead" (Phil. 3:10–11). Paul wrote, "I also consider everything to be a loss in view of the surpassing value of knowing Christ Jesus my Lord" (Phil. 3:8).

Great glory comes to God when His people suffer in faith and grasp the victory that is there. When Jesus knelt in Gethsemane and anticipated the suffering and agony of the cross, He prayed, "Father, the hour has come. Glorify Your Son, so that your Son may glorify You" (John 17:1). The apostle Paul also knew of this glory. He wrote, "I consider that the sufferings of this present time are not worth comparing with the glory that is going to be revealed to us" (Rom. 8:18).

Days of hopelessness and helplessness will come, but we will find comfort in the words of Jesus: "I have told you these things so that in Me you may have peace. You will have suffering in this world. Be courageous! I have conquered the world" (John 16:33).

When the storm surrounds us, we can hear the voice of God in the whirlwind and learn the victory of faith and the value of repentance. We have ready access to God whenever we turn to Him. 1 John 1:9 says, "If we confess our sins, He is faithful and just to forgive us our sins and to cleanse us from all unrighteousness." When we turn to God, He will give us an inner witness that we are His children, and we will know that we have eternal life. "And this is the testimony: God has given us eternal life, and this life is in His Son. The one who has the Son has life. The one who doesn't have the Son of God does not have life" (1 John 5:11–12). God does not want anyone to perish; He desires us all to turn to Him in repentance (2 Pet. 3:9).

Jim Elliot, one of the missionaries killed by the Auca Indians, kept a journal. Prior to his death he entered words that have become a challenge to millions: "He is no fool to give what he cannot keep to gain what he cannot lose." The message of the book of Job is the same. God does not necessarily give us what we want when we cry out in distress or despair. Instead of giving what would provide momentary satisfaction, he gives us something upon which we can build our lives: He gives us lessons in the victory of faith and the value of contrition. We learn that we can reach through the darkness and touch the hand of Him who lives forever; in the midst of our hopelessness we can hear the voice of God.

Chapter 5

Born for Trouble

Job 5:6–7

Trouble is on its way, and we cannot stop it. It is the universal experience of mankind. In the speech recorded in Job 5, Eliphaz declared that humans are born for trouble. He told his friend Job that trouble does not come to just a few; it is normal. Eliphaz said. "For distress does not grow out of the soil, and trouble does not sprout from the ground. But mankind is born for trouble as surely as sparks fly upward" (Job 5:6–7).

Eliphaz concluded that only if there were no human beings would the world be free from trouble. Hopeless resignation gripped him. He attributed all trouble to humans, as if God were somehow not in control.

Job, on the other hand, linked his trouble to God. Although he did not accuse God of causing his trouble directly, he acknowledged that God was somehow in the midst of his difficulties. Job did not view his suffering as aimless; he was not hopeless. Answering Eliphaz in Job 6, Job argued that God was working in and through his trouble: "Surely the arrows of the Almighty have pierced me ... God's terrors are arrayed against me" (Job 6:4).

Sometimes everything seems to be arrayed against us. Just when we think we "have it made," something bad happens. When we get that fixed, something else bad happens. When it rains, it pours. Yet sometimes we discover that those troubles are really blessings in disguise; they are instruments God uses to bless us. He allows difficulties so that He can accomplish particular purposes or achieve particular goals in our lives.

Sometimes God allows trouble to enter the lives of sinners because He wants to redeem them. Sometimes God allows trouble to enter the lives of believers in order to refine them. Sometimes God allows trouble to enter the lives of His servants because He seeks to rekindle them.

God Wants to Redeem Sinners

Many people are too affluent, comfortable, or busy to be bothered with God. Even if they occasionally acknowledge that they need God, they occupy themselves with other things that keep them from thinking about Him. They ignore him when He says, "'Come, let us discuss this,' says the Lord, 'Though your sins are like scarlet, they will be as white as snow; though they are as red as crimson, they will be like wool'" (Isa. 1:18). Some people are unwilling to take time to think about eternity or worship God.

Our word *worship* comes from the Old English terns *worth* and *ship*, which together indicate "the condition of deserving, or being held in, esteem or repute; honor, distinction, renown; good name, credit."[1] A call to worship asks a person to stop doing whatever he is doing and to prostrate himself in reverence and homage. The object of worship commands complete attention and devotion.

The reason so few of us worship is that we never stop doing what we are doing. Our minds are constantly thinking and planning. Although many of us attend worship services, our minds tend to wander because we do not shift gears when we enter the church.

Because it is difficult for preoccupied Christians to listen to and consider the call of God, He sometimes allows trouble to come into their lives in order to get their attention. God also allows trouble to come into the lives of lost people to get their attention.

For example, God sent trouble to wicked King Manasseh. The Bible says, "Manasseh was 12 years old when he became king; he reigned 55 years in Jerusalem. He did what was evil in the Lord's sight." (2 Chron. 33:1–2). Manasseh did everything wrong. He set up idols and altars for the worship of Baal. He corrupted the worship of Jehovah by mixing the worship of God with the worship of pagan idols. His reign was a low-water mark in the history of the Jewish people. "Manasseh caused Judah and the inhabitants of Jerusalem to stray so that they did worse evil than the nations the Lord had destroyed before the Israelites." (2 Chron. 33:9).

Manasseh did not have time for God during his prosperous years. He was busy playing God, achieving compromises, and accomplishing mischief. Then God sent the Assyrians to conquer the people of God and take Manasseh into captivity, and Manasseh turned to the Lord. "When he was in distress, he sought the favor of the Lord his God and earnestly humbled himself before the God of his ancestors. He prayed to Him, so He heart his petition and granted his requres … So Manasseh came to know that the Lord is God" (2 Chron. 33:12–13). This Old Testament story shows that God sometimes allows trouble to come into the life of a lost person in order to get his attention.

An example from the New Testament is the prodigal son (Luke 15:11–32). When he left home, he was arrogant, self-righteous, self-sufficient, self-confident, and determined to do things his own way. He did not have time for God, and he refused to listen to his father or anyone else. For a while he lived well, but then he ran out of money and ended up in a pigpen. Finally his thoughts turned to his father, who lovingly welcomed him home. The prodigal had to get to the bottom before he could look up. Sometimes God allows trouble to bring us to the bottom so we will look up to Him. Trouble reveals that we are not self-sufficient; we are not adequate to meet the challenges of life without the Lord.

God used trouble to get the attention of Chuck Colson. As President Nixon's hatchet man, Colson wielded power and influence. He was known to be a cold, ruthless, and heartless individual who would have run over his own grandmother if she got in the way. Colson thought he was self-sufficient and did not need God. Then he became involved in the Watergate scandal and ended up in a federal penitentiary. In prison he reached the lowest point of his life.

He had to get down to look up. In prison he found the time to turn his attention to God and through the faithful witness of a few of his friends, Chuck Colson was saved. Now an eloquent spokesman for the Christian faith, he has written several books that present the gospel of Jesus Christ. God allowed reversals and disappointments in his life for the purpose of redeeming him.

God Wants to Refine Believers

As Christians we are all in the process of being refined. Receiving Jesus Christ as Savior is just the beginning of our spiritual lives. God has not finished His work in us when we are saved. He desires to make us like Jesus, and sometimes He uses adversity to achieve His goal.

Often we Christians feel as if everything is pitted against us. Sometimes circumstances hedge us in and we can see no way out of our difficulties. We realize we need God's help to get us through our ordeals.

God allows us to face difficulties in order to refine and sanctify us. *Sanctify* is a theological term meaning "to set apart, to make holy." Any person, place, or object that is sanctified is set apart from common or secular use and is dedicated to God's use. For the Christian, sanctification is the process that God uses to make us like Jesus.

God sets us apart for Himself, and He is in the process of conforming us to the image of His Son. The apostle Paul wrote: "We know that all things work together for the good of those who love God: those who are called according to His purpose. For those He foreknew He also predestined to be conformed to the image of His Son, so that He would be the firstborn among many brothers" (Rom. 8:28–29). This great truth appears in the midst of a passage dealing with trouble and follows Romans 7 where Paul spoke of the conflict all Christians experience because we are not yet like Christ: "For I do not do the god that I want to do, but I practice the evil that I do not want to do" (Rom. 7:19). Troubles work together for our good, then, because God uses them to transform us into the likeness of Jesus Christ.

Nothing happens by chance. Everything that happens comes by the permissive will of God. He does not cause it all, but He allows it to happen. Everything in our lives is within the scope of His understanding and permission. What He allows will serve the purpose of our sanctification.

Jesus told His disciples, "Remember the word I spoke to you: 'A slave is not greater than his master.' If they persecuted Me, they will also persecute you" (John 15:20). Hebrews 2:10 says, "For it was fitting, in bringing many sons to glory, that He, for whom and through whom all things exist, should make the source of their salvation perfect through sufferings." Jesus Christ became the "payment in full" for our sin. He perfectly fulfilled the demands of holiness from a righteous God. Yet even His sacrifice was perfected through suffering. If we are to be like the Master, we must be refined in the fires of trouble, testing, and difficulty.

Hebrews 12:5 speaks of "the Lord's discipline" and verse 6 says, "For the Lord disciplines the one He loves." When God chastens us, He is disciplining us to help us grow up in Him. Because He loves us, He uses chastisement to discourage us from doing anything that might hinder us from being conformed to the image of Jesus. Verses 10 and 11 go on to say that our human fathers "disciplined us for a short time based on what seemed good to them, but He does it for our benefit, so that we can share His holiness. No discipline seems enjoyable at the time, but painful. Later on, however, it yields the fruit of peace and righteousness to those who have been trained by it."

It is not enjoyable to go through troubled times. It is difficult to endure the pressure of disappointment and discipline. But our troubles shrink into insignificance when we think of the long-term results and God's great purpose in allowing difficulties. God's purpose is to make us like the Master. What God sets out to do, He will accomplish. Our all-knowing and all-powerful God is able to achieve His purpose. Nothing can defeat His work in our lives.

The psalmist reflected on the work of affliction in his life when he wrote, "Before I was afflicted I went astray, But now I keep Your word" (Ps. 119:67). Many of us have a similar testimony. When everything went our way, we drifted from God. When trouble came, we turned back to God. Trouble often draws us to Him and causes us to reflect on His love for us and His will for our lives. This reflection, in turn, causes us to commit ourselves anew to Him.

Zechariah prophesied about the refining process that the children of Israel will endure: "The Lord's declaration—'In the whole land two-thirds will be cut off and die, but a third will be left in it. I will put this third through the fire; I will refine them as silver is refined and test them as gold is tested. They will call on My name, and I will answer them. I will say: They are My people, and they will say: The Lord is our God'" (Zech. 13:8–9). After being troubled, tried, and tested in the refining fire, God's people will call on His name. And when God allows trouble to come to believers today, it always results in their refinement.

God Wants to Rekindle Our Devotion

Trouble can also reignite the fire of our love for God. Sometimes God allows His servants to face trouble for the purpose of rekindling them. God has many children He is not able to use because they have let their love cool and their interest in the things of God fade. They think they can get along without him. Saved, comfortable, and self-satisfied, they work for God as long as it is convenient. They do not realize that spiritual work is not our working for God, but God working through us. Because they do not understand what God's work is all about, they endeavor to use and manipulate God.

It is a sad situation when we as God's children become so calloused and apathetic that we do not realize how much God wants to use us. In order to help us recognize that fact, He often allows trouble to come into our lives.

God wanted to use Simon Peter, but his usefulness needed to be rekindled. Knowing that Peter would have to go through a time of trouble before he could be used effectively, Jesus said, "Simon, Simon, look out! Satan has asked to sift you like wheat. But I have prayed for you that your faith may not fail. And you, when you have turned back, strengthen your brothers" (Luke 22:31–32). Jesus did not pray that Peter would not be sifted. He prayed that Peter's faith would survive the sifting and that after his testing he would strengthen his brothers.

Peter thought that he was ready to go to prison and die for Jesus. How self-sufficient and arrogant he was! Without divine empowering, Peter was too weak to withstand the pressures he would face. Jesus said, "I tell you, Peter, the rooster will not crow today until you deny three times that you know Me!" (Luke 22:34). Three times that night Peter denied Jesus. He failed His Lord and then "went outside and wept bitterly" (Luke 22:62).

After Peter was sifted and tried, God was able to use him. On the day of Pentecost, Peter preached a powerful sermon and three thousand people were saved (Acts 2:41). God used him mightily after he had gotten rid of his pride.

God wants to use us, in Peter's words, to "proclaim the praises of the One who called you out of darkness into His marvelous light" (1 Pet. 2:9). But some of us God does not use because we are so sure we can serve Him in our own strength. Independent self-confidence is not a characteristic that God can use, so He may allow trouble to come into our lives to remove our pride.

Job understood that God had sent trouble into his life to rekindle his usefulness. "Yet He knows the way I have taken; when He has tested me, I will emerge as pure gold" (Job 23:10). Anything that God has to do to rekindle our commitment to Him is worthwhile. Anything that drives us to our knees is good for us.

God, who is always in control of what is happening, permits things to affect us so that He can carry out His greater plan. For example, what happened to Joseph refined and rekindled him and made him useful to God in carrying out His plan for His chosen people. Joseph was hated by his brothers, sold into slavery, and taken to Egypt, where he was falsely accused and jailed. He remained faithful to God in spite of his circumstances, however, and after his release from prison he rose to a pinnacle of power in ancient Egypt. In that position he was able to provide grain for his family during a time of famine. Thus Joseph's trouble made him useful to God in preserving the children of Israel.

Whenever trouble, disappointment, or discouragement comes, we who are God's children can be sure that He has allowed it. He uses it as a tool to refine us, rekindle us, and make us usable in His service. Our response to trouble reflects our attitude and predisposition. One option is to respond with bitterness, anger, and resentment. The other option is to bow before God and submit to Him and His refining process. If we submit to the refining process, our devotion to God will be rekindled and we will become useful vessels committed to His service. Like Job, we will be able to say, "The Lord gives, and the Lord takes away. Praise the name of the Lord" (Job 1:21). God is still in control, and we can acknowledge that He still knows the way by following Him.

If our hearts are open to the refining process, we can be free from bitterness, the most treacherous master the world has ever known. If we submit to our loving Master, we will emerge as gold.

Our works will be tried by fire at the judgment seat of Christ. The works that were based on selfish motives will be consumed like wood, hay, and stubble. Other works will survive like gold, silver, and precious stones (1 Cor. 3:11–15).

As we have seen, God allows trouble to come into the lives of sinners in order to redeem them. He allows trouble to come into the lives of saints in order to refine them. He also allows trouble to come into the lives of His servants in order to rekindle their love for Him. During trials and troubles, we can respond by turning to God or reacting against Him. He promises that if we turn to Him, He will not turn us away. He also promises to mold and develop us into the very image of our Lord and Savior Jesus Christ. The options are clear, and the choice is left to us.

Endnotes

1 *Oxford English Dictionary.*

Chapter 6

Songs in the Night

Job 35:10–11

During times of trouble we need encouragement. We need positive reinforcement—about our own worth and our relationship to others. Elihu's magnificent speech is a marvelous encouragement for believers who are experiencing difficulties. His words provide us with assurance as they witness to God's presence in our stressful circumstances.

Elihu's speech appears after a lengthy series of discourses by Job's three friends—Eliphaz, Bildad, and Zophar—and Job's summary defense. When Job finished his last speech, Elihu stepped forward and gave his perspective on their speeches. Then Elihu spoke of those going through "severe oppression" (Job 35:9). It was obvious to him that God was working in their lives. Reflecting on their dark circumstances he said, "God … provides us with songs in the night" (Job 35:10). Whenever things are darkest, God is present!

The Bible employs the imagery of nighttime to represent suffering, sorrow, struggle, sin, and defeat. Nighttime has the same symbolic meanings in secular literature. We ourselves view the night as a time of deep personal encounters. When the telephone rings or someone knocks on the door in the darkness of the night, we are filled with dread. Or we may associate nighttime with the loneliness that can overwhelm us as we stare out into the blackness. And we may think of being kept awake at night by burning consciences or afflictions. The idea of singing songs in any of these situations seems ludicrous at first.

The best the world can do in times of distress is whistle. Nearly all of us can remember mustering a whistle when we were frightened of the dark. But a Christian has something better than a whistle or human wisdom to stir up his courage. The person who walks with his hand in the hand of the Lord has a better resource: he has the Spirit of the Lord filling his life. When we anchor our faith in God, we never walk alone. God our Maker gives us songs in the night instead of a whistle to help us through life's difficult circumstances.

During nighttime experiences, the greatest cause of distress among Christians is a faulty sense of direction. We try to avoid struggles and suffering instead of looking to the Lord. We do not have songs in the night because we do not ask the preliminary question, "Where is God my Maker ...?" (Job 35:10). This question does not suggest doubt about the existence of God or His involvement in our lives. The question calls us to set our "direction finder" on God. We need to look to God rather than our circumstances for songs in the night.

One illustration of how God provides for us in dire circumstances is the story of Elisha and his servant at Dothan. One night the king of Syria's army surrounded the city in order to capture them. Elisha's servant woke up early and saw their distressful situation. He went to Elisha and said, "Oh, my master, what are we to do?" (2 Kgs. 6:15).

Elisha replied, "Don't be afraid, for those who are with us outnumber those who are with them" (2 Kgs. 6:16).

Then the Lord opened the servant's eyes and he saw that "the mountain was covered with horses and chariots of fire all around Elisha" (2 Kgs. 6:17). God had already prepared the victory for His servants. All they needed to do was look to God. The servant needed to have the same sense of direction Elisha had. Oh, that we might have the right sense of direction when our circumstances overwhelm us in the darkness and shadows of the night!

Elihu pointed out, "No one says, 'Where is God my Maker, Who provides us with songs in the night …?'" (Job 35:10). It is tragic that we often try everything but God to help us cope difficulties. During the night of sin and defeat, we tend to look for ways to avoid the consequences of our actions instead of looking to the Lord to rescue us.

Anyone can sing in the daytime when the notes can be seen in the light. But in order to sing in the nighttime we must have a confidence that overrides the darkness of doubt and the shadows of despair. Such confidence does not come naturally. It is a special gift from God. In the darkness when we cannot see the notes, we must focus on God in praise and gratitude so that we can sing from our hearts.

God enabled Peter to "sing" in times of distress and persecution. King Herod, who persecuted the early church in Jerusalem, killed James the brother of John and arrested Peter. Peter was in danger of being executed, but he did not fret about his circumstances. He slept soundly in his prison. Why was he able to face his pending trial so calmly? Because he had experienced Pentecost. He was empowered by God the Holy Spirit to focus his "direction finder" on God his Maker. Acts 12:6–8 reveals how God intervened on Peter's behalf:

> On the night before Herod was to bring him out for execution, Peter was sleeping between two soldiers, bound with two chains, while the sentries in front of the door guarded the prison. Suddenly an angel of the Lord appeared, and a light shone in the cell. Striking Peter on the side, he woke him up and said, "Quick, get up!" Then the chains fell of his wrists. "Get dressed," the angel told him, "and put on your sandals." And he did so. "Wrap your cloak around you," he told him, "and follow me."

Paul and Silas were given literal songs in the night. They were in dire circumstances, for after the Holy Spirit guided them to Macedonia, they were beaten and imprisoned at Philippi. Luke described the situation:

> Then the mob joined in the attack against them, and the chief magistrates stripped off their clothes and ordered them to be beaten with rods. After they had inflicted many blows on them, they threw them in jail, ordering the jailer to keep them securely guarded. Receiving such an order, he put them into the inner prison and secured their feet in stocks. About midnight Paul and Silas were praying and singing hymns to God, and the prisoners were listening to them (Acts 16:22–25).

Paul and Silas were the victims of mob violence, magisterial abuse, corporal punishment, and strict confinement. How could they sing at midnight? They could sing because they had their "direction finder" focused on God their Maker. God gave them songs, and He also gave them deliverance and a harvest of souls. Salvation came to some who had contributed to their distress—the jailer and his household. What a wonderful Savior we serve!

We need to learn to sing songs in the night, for has there ever been a day darker than our day? Have we ever had a time of worldwide terror, global economic collapse, loss of jobs, destruction of savings and retirement funds, violence, and tragedy more than today? Has there ever been a time when we needed to experience God's deliverance more than we do today? Has there ever been a time when the church was assaulted the way it is today? We hear much talk about religion today, but we see little evidence of real faith. We hear a great deal about the outward signs of faith but very little about the heart of faith. We are urged to focus on our circumstances instead of on God our Maker. The downfall of prominent Christian leaders reminds us that every believer is under attack by Satan and his hosts.

Satan is doing all he can to neutralize the church. Believing that there is already enough apathy and indifference in the church to render it ineffective, he seeks to rob the church of its leaders. Satan assumes that if he can destroy those who spearhead the work of the church in the world, he can defeat the church in this age. In this time of tremendous assault we need to find songs in the night.

The Source of the Songs

The source of the songs is God. We know from Job 35:10 that God is the giver of songs in the night. They belong to God alone. We may try to sing apart from God, but we cannot. We cannot make a song of grace fit into a nighttime setting of grief.

Where is the source? In Elihu's words, "Where is God my Maker, Who provides us with songs in the night … ?" He is omnipresent; that is, He is present everywhere in all His fullness at every instant. What a wonderful truth! Zophar asked, "Can you fathom the depths of God or discover the limits of the Almighty? They are higher than the heavens … they are deeper than Sheol … Their measure is longer than the earth And wider than the sea" (Job 11:7–9). God is wherever we are. Nothing "will have the power to separate us from the love of God that is in Christ Jesus our Lord!" (Rom. 8:39).

God is also omnipotent. He is able to do anything that is needed to deliver His children from their situations or to bring them through their circumstances. Yet we tend to take God for granted. Our tendency is not to give God his due respect. While most of us think it would be unconscionable not to give each person his or her due respect, we tend to ignore and neglect God. We rob Him of honor, praise, thanksgiving, and obedience. Yet He is the source of the songs we need in life's nighttimes. Elihu's words call us to turn to God who alone can give songs of victory in dark times of pressure and sadness.

The Essence of the Songs

Music is a universal language. In every culture music touches the soul. The words of music touch the heart even more deeply than words of theology. When truth is put to music it reaches out and touches us for eternity. Many of the great teachings of Christianity have been passed on from generation to generation in the words of songs and hymns that God has given us through His grace. We can understand why Ephesians 5:18–20 instructs us to "be filled with the Spirit, speaking to one another in psalms, hymns and spiritual songs, singing and making music to the Lord in your heart, giving thanks always for everything to God the Father in the name of our Lord Jesus Christ."

In His grace, God has given us intellect. Job 35:11 says that He "gives us more understanding than the animals of the earth and makes us wiser than the birds of the sky." Not by accident, but by design, man was created with the capacity to reason and respond to God by intelligent choice. Therefore we can sing the songs God gives if we choose to sing them. If we open our hearts to Him, we can experience His presence and power in the midst of troublesome circumstances. To the animal kingdom, suffering is pointless. But intelligent human beings who are meant to trust in God can find meaning in pain. We can know the reality of God in the midst of it.

The songs God gives in the night speak of His grace—the unmerited favor He has bestowed on us. God is our instructor, and if we do not understand the grace of God, it is because we choose not to understand it. If we choose not to hear the songs God gives, we will not be able to sing them.

The Setting of the Songs

The setting of these songs of grace is grief. During times of grief our hearts take the place of our eyes: "We walk by faith, not by sight" (2 Cor. 5:7). Although we cannot see the light, we can sense the presence of God.

Although the sky is dark, we are not afraid or dismayed. Although there is no light to guide us, we are not without direction. Although there is no opening in the clouds and no dividing of the gloom that surrounds us, we are not distraught. A midnight song is a powerful witness to our faith.

Paul wrote, "Now we have this treasure in clay jars, so that this extraordinary power may be from God and not from us. We are pressured in every way but not crushed; we are perplexed but not in despair; we are persecuted but not abandoned; we are struck down but not destroyed" (2 Cor. 4:7–9). Because Christ is in our lives, our hearts find a way to sing in spite of dire circumstances. Like Paul and Silas, we believers have songs in the night. At the darkest moment, God's song pierces the gloom and becomes a substitute for sunshine. Each Christian can testify, "Even when I go through the darkest valley, I fear no danger, for You are with me; Your rod and Your staff—they comfort me" (Ps. 23:4).

Singing has a great effect on those who sing and those who hear the singing. Think again of Paul and Silas singing at midnight in the Philippian jail. As the notes floated through the dungeon, the other prisoners were probably awestruck by the holy and heavenly music. The refreshing and uplifting songs must have drawn them toward God, moved them spiritually, and impacted their behavior, for when the earthquake opened doors and loosed chains, the prisoners did not flee. "When the jailer woke up and saw the doors of the prison open, he drew his sword and was going to kill himself, since he thought the prisoners had escaped. But Paul called out with a loud voice, 'Don't harm yourself, because all of us are here!'" (Acts 16:27–28). God had used the songs in the night to prepare the hearts of the prisoners.

What a great moment it is when we learn to sing the songs He gives! We can learn if we want to. If we want God, we can have Him. If we desire grace and strength, we can have them. No matter how deep our grief, He is always ready to lift our hearts. No matter how dark the setting, God is always there to provide salvation and forgiveness. If we entrust our hearts and souls to Him, we will never again have to ask, "Where is God?" We will know that He lives within us.

The Subject of the Songs

Charles Haddon Spurgeon said, "When we sing by night, there are three things we can sing about. Either sing about the day that is over, or about the night itself, or else about the morrow that is to come."[1] What a song!

We can sing about the past. It may be dark now, but we can remember when God moved into our lives—when daylight came with the stirring of our souls in faith. We can remember the unforgettable moments when God spoke to our hearts, when God burst through our understanding and made Himself known to us. When we stumble and fall, we can remember the past: God was always there to pick us up, cleanse us, and forgive us. We can sing about the things He did in "the day that is over." God has made a difference in our lives, and in the night we can sing about the past when God was so real in our lives.

We can also sing about the night. No matter how dark it is, it could be darker. We can thank God that we are not consumed by the darkness. "Because of the Lord's faithful love we do not perish, for His mercies never end" (Lam. 3:22). When God allows the night to surround us, He also gives us the ability and the opportunity to sing His song of triumph. Whatever our circumstances are, Lamentations 3:23–24 can be our hymn: "Great is Your faithfulness … The Lord is my portion … Therefore I will put my hope in Him!"

Then we can sing about tomorrow. The day will come when the Lord God omnipotent will reign perfectly in all the universe and the night of despair that shrouds our hearts will vanish. We can sing about that day because the purposes of God will not be defeated by the darkness. In the solar system, darkness covers one side of a planet, while light floods the other side. Likewise in our personal lives we may be in darkness for a little while, but the darkness will pass and the brightness will come again. The darkness that often engulfs us with its fears and frustrations will dissipate, and we will enter into full light forever and ever. In the night that now surrounds us, we can sing of the day that is coming.

God loves to hear His people sing in the night. He rejoices when our hearts reach out to Him in praise, faith, and adoration. And as we focus on our Father, we will experience delight and exuberant joy. Our hope in Him provides us with a way to make sense of the darkness, and we can emerge from it with victory.

The non-Christian who focuses on his grief will be filled with despair. The Christian's focus on God does not eliminate his grief, but his attitude of trust fills him with hope in the midst of sorrow and he can sing songs in the night. His songs witness to a world that has no song that there is a God who gives grace and mercy. Singing is the best recommendation of his faith he can give.

The world needs a song now more than ever, for the darkness of apathy prevails. There are enough believers in America to Christianize the world, but we cannot accomplish that task because we are mired in the bog of indifference. Many Christians turn their attention to God on Sunday and forget about Him the rest of the week. They do not seem to understand that the God they worship on Sunday is the God who wants to give them songs in the night. Some people attend church activities, but outside of church they act as if there were no God; they lie, cheat, steal, and commit adultery just as the ungodly do. How dark is the night that surrounds us!

Psalm 46:1–3 says: "God is our refuge and strength, a helper who is always found in times of trouble. Therefore we will not be afraid, though the earth trembles and the mountains topple into the depths of the seas, though its waters roar and foam and the mountains quake with its turmoil." The One who is our "helper … in times of trouble" (Ps. 46:1) is to be praised publicly and privately. He deserves our worship in public, and He deserves our trust in the night. God gives us songs in the night so we can praise Him in the night. But we can only hear those songs when, after having come to God in genuine repentance and faith, we focus on our Maker.

Endnotes

1 Charles Haddon Spurgeon, *Metropolitan Tabernacle Pulpit* (Pasadena, TX: Pilgrim Publications, 1976) 44:100.

Chapter 7

With Friends Like You, Who Needs Enemies?

Job 16:1–5

Sometimes well-meaning friends do more harm than good. They may have good intentions, but their efforts create problems. Job had three such friends.

We first encounter these three friends in Job 2. Having heard about Job's troubles, they were moved with compassion and wanted to do something about his plight. They left their homes and went to visit Job with the intention of bringing encouragement by mourning with him and comforting him in his time of sorrow.

When Job's friends arrived, they were unprepared for what they found. Job was near death, and his appearance was so pitiful that at first they did not even recognize him. They probably agreed with his wife that death would be the best thing for him. But according to the customs of that day, they sat down with him for seven days and nights. They were expressing their concern for Job in the best way they knew.

The three men seemed compassionate, and they were going what they thought was appropriate. They listened to Job's lament (Job 3) and then each of them—Eliphaz, Bildad, and Zophar—spoke about what he felt was the underlying problem. Their compassion, however, turned to accusation as they addressed Job's condition. Their speeches and Job's responses are recorded in Job 4–14. Eliphaz made a second speech (Job 15), and Job 16 contains Job's reply to Eliphaz in particular and all three friends in general.

Job could not fail to recognize the change in his friends' attitude. He said of them "You coat the truth with lies you are all worthless doctors" (Job 13:4) and "You are all miserable comforters" (Job 16:2). A good paraphrase would read, "With friends like you, who needs enemies?"

Job's friends came to comfort him, but the fact is that they afflicted him. They came to encourage him, but they actually added to his despair. They came to heal, but they only made his condition worse. They brought more woe than good. Their shift in attitude has become notorious. Even today when we want to refer to people who torment us instead of encouraging us, we call them "Job's comforters." This derisive term applies to people who hurt instead of help.

We can learn lessons about friendship from the example of Eliphaz, Bildad, and Zophar. We can look at what they did right and what they did wrong.

Lessons about Friendship

How much we need friendship! Friendship is a missing ingredient in much of modern American Christianity. Today Christianity in America is largely a spectator sport. All too often we attend church to observe. We do not want to become involved or committed in church activities. We seem to be dedicated to the good times and not to the work of building friendships. Paradoxically, most of us would have to admit that our number one problem is loneliness. In fact, surveys show that the deepest problem in American society today in loneliness. We are lonely because we do not have friends. We do not have friends because we do not know how to be friends.

Friendship is a godly, biblical concept. Love is the hedge of discipleship for the followers of Jesus Christ (John 13:35). Everyone needs someone to trust and lean on when things go wrong, but not everyone knows how to have friends or be a friend. Friendship requires taking time to build relationships—to build trust and love. We can follow the example of Job's friends in devoting time to a friendship.

The Lesson about Time

Job's friends started out well. They were right to want to encourage their friend. Their intentions were good, and their efforts were considerable. Eliphaz, Bildad, and Zophar spent a lot of time with Job. They stayed with him seven days and seven nights before they said anything to him. Time is the most precious thing one person can give to another. In our day we are generally too busy to give the time required to get involved with people and build friendships.

The Lesson about Compassion

Job's friends grieved with him—they shared his sorrow. They hurt for their famous, well-educated, upright friend. They sympathized with him in his time of distress. When they saw his extensive disfigurement, their hearts were torn and they wept over him. They were men of compassion. That was good.

Many of today's congregations are dry-eyed. We have seen and heard of so much distress and destruction on the evening news that we have become calloused—insensitive to pain and suffering. It would do us good to weep over the distress of others. Jesus wept when He looked at the tomb of His friend Lazarus (John 11:35), and we too need to demonstrate compassion.

Do you love someone enough to weep for him? If you do, you are a valuable friend.

The Lesson about Comfort

Job's friends comforted him. When they sat with him for seven days and nights, they grieved and wept with him but did not say anything. They were willing to be quiet and let him suffer without adding to his suffering. They were a solace to him in his hour of need. Eliphaz, Bildad, and Zophar did well up to that point.

There are times when words are useless. What can one say to a person who is in the hospital on a respirator and has less than a day to live? Sometimes the best thing we can do is just be there. Silence is a wonderful gift. Most of us, however, are enamored by the sound of our own voices, and we sometimes speak when we should be quiet. Maybe the best thing we can do for someone in distress is put our arms around him and cry with him.

In Job 2, Job's friends set good examples for us to follow as we seek to respond to the needs of others. However, their approach deteriorated rapidly because of their lack of understanding.

The Lesson about Understanding

Everything was going well until Job told his friends about his difficulties (Job 3). When Job opened his mouth and told Eliphaz, Bildad, and Zophar how he felt, they began to make accusations. Job's friends heard his words, but they did not hear his heart. They heard his words but missed their meaning. Although Job questioned God, he never accused Him. His friends were not able to understand that his expression of anger and frustration was not an attack on God. They did not hear the spiritual heartbeat of Job. They did not recognize the grief and turmoil in his heart.

Job's friends were faced with a situation that seemed to contradict their theology. Job had the same theology and the same conflict, and he was beginning to have doubts. He began to question his doctrines. Since his friends valued their theology more than they valued Job, they chose to abandon him rather than walk with him through his search for answers. They forsook Job instead of helping him come to grips with the reality of God in a life filled with doubt and despair. They could not reach out to their friend in his need.

At first Job's friends only hinted that perhaps he was a sinner and God was punishing him because of his sin. They suggested that he repent of his sin and seek God. When hints did not work, they made direct accusations. For example, Zophar no longer only insinuated that Job was misrepresenting his situation; Zophar accused him of lying. It was much easier for Job's friends to accuse him than to help their beleaguered companion work through his problems. When the three men made their accusations, they showed that their compassion was not genuine. Sometimes when we do not understand a friend's behavior, we too find it easier to accuse him than to take the time to help him work through his difficulties.

Later Eliphaz accused Job of specific sins: "For you took collateral from your brothers without cause, stripping off their clothes and leaving them naked. You gave no water to the thirsty and withheld food from the famished, while the land belonged to a powerful man and an influential man lived on it. You sent widows away empty-handed, and the strength of the fatherless was crushed" (Job 22:6–9). Then Bildad accused Job of being a terrible person: "How can a person be justified before God? ... If even the moon does not shine and the stars are not pure in His sight, how much less man, who is a maggot, and the son of man, who is a worm?" (Job 25:4–6).

These direct accusations demonstrated that Job's friends were not especially sympathetic to what he was going through. They were not able to adjust their thinking and their opinions to the realistic situation.

In the distress of the circumstances, their theology broke down. Their stiff and cold doctrines overcame their discretion.

When direct accusations proved ineffective in convincing Job of his sin, Zophar said to him, "God has chosen to overlook some of your sin" (Job 11:6). Resorting to biting sarcasm, the frustrated Eliphaz asked Job, "Does it delight the Almighty if you are righteous?" (Job 22:3). In other words, "Is God better off because you are righteous?"

Job's friends' approach deteriorated from sarcasm to lies and misrepresentations. They were so far off base that Job said, "You coat the truth with lies; you are all worthless doctors. If only you would shut up and let that be your wisdom!" (Job 13:4–5).

Harsh, cruel, malicious, and unfeeling in their response to a grieving father, Job's friends said that God killed his children because they had sinned (Job 8:4). No wonder Job said, "I have heard many things like these. You are all miserable comforters. Is there no end to your empty words? What provokes you that you continue testifying?" (Job 16:2–3).

Unfortunately, we sometimes fail to understand our friends too. We are quick to believe the worst about the people we respect the most. Our criticisms are often couched in harsh words. We seem to forget that Jesus said, "Do not judge, so that you won't be judged. For with the judgment you use, you will be judged, and with the measure you use, it will be measured to you" (Matt. 7:1–2). What goes around comes around. We are going to get what we give.

Much trouble in the Christian world today comes from our not being willing to obey the word of God in relation to our Christian brothers and sisters. We often look for ways to misrepresent the statements of our friends and to condemn what they do. We judge their motives although we cannot see their hearts. Sometimes we even enjoy making accusations; we gain a false sense of importance when we attack someone. Although we desperately need friends, we may lose ours because we do not understand how to treat them.

The Lesson about Attitudes

The visit of Job's friends started out well, but then their attitudes changed. They began to think they were better than Job. Eliphaz based his feelings of superiority on experience: note his use of the phrase "I have seen" in Job 15:17. He argued from the perspective of an elder statesman who thought his experience gave him the right to judge (Job 15:10). Bildad kept referring to past generations as he spoke. He felt his arguments were superior because they were based more on tradition and history than on personal experience. Zophar, the youngest of the three friends, based his arguments on mere assumptions. He did not appeal to experience or tradition. He felt his personal opinions were superior, and as a result his arguments were harsh.

Many people today are like Zophar. Like him, they assume certain things to be true. They are opinionated and don't feel that they have to give reasons for their opinions. They merely pass judgment and think that their friends should accept their views without question.

Job's friends had good intentions, but they did not have the characteristics of true friends. They wanted to help Job in his time of trouble, but they were judgmental rather than accepting. The characteristics of a true friend are found in the following description:

A Portrait of a Friend

When things don't come out right, he comes right in.
When none of your dreams come true, he is.
He never looks for your money except when you have lost it.
He never gets in your way except to clear it for you.
Nothing is more important to him than making you important.
He is in your corner when you are cornered.
He turns up when you get turned down.
All he wants in return for his helping hand is your handshake.

He raps your critics when they are wrong and takes the rap for you when they are right.

You can do anything you want with his friendship except buy it or sell it.

He makes you realize that having a real friend is like having an extra life.[1]

Job's friends did not understand the principles of friendship; they did not understand that being a true friend involves unselfishness, loyalty, honesty, and commitment.

Principles of Friendship

A Friend Is Unselfish

A true friend loves unselfishly. We read about unselfish love in 1 Samuel 20:17: "Jonathan once again swore to David in his love for him, because he loved him as he loved himself." Jesus spoke of this kind of love when he said, "No one has greater love than this, that someone would lay down his life for his friends" (John 15:13).

When we love unselfishly, we are willing to give ourselves, our time, and even our reputations. We are willing to love sacrificially—that is, we do not require others to respond in kind. God loved the world sacrificially (John 3:16) and the world responded with hatred (John 17:14).

A Friend Is Loyal

None of us is perfect, so we cannot demand perfection in others. But we can be loyal to one another. Loyalty is the most prized quality of a friend. It is dedication based on acceptance and love. A friend will be your advocate before presuming to be your judge. He will come to your defense before accusing you. You can know how many friends you have by counting your advocates and your judges.

The book of Proverbs is filled with references to loyalty. For example, Proverbs 18:24 says, "There is a friend who stays closer than a brother." A loyal friend will stick with you even in adversity. Providing a contrast, Proverbs 25:19 says, "Trusting an unreliable person in a time of trouble is like a rotten tooth or a faltering foot." Trusting someone who is not loyal is like running a race on a broken ankle or eating a raw apple with a broken tooth. It can be done, but it is difficult.

The Bible gives us many examples of disloyal friends. Samson's friend Delilah caused him great distress and personal injury. Uriah's friend David used Uriah's loyalty for his own selfish purpose. The pharaoh's butler was Joseph's friend when times were tough, but when things were going well he did not remember Joseph. With false friends such as these, who needs enemies?

People can be friendly without being friends. There is a difference between acquaintances and friends. We have many acquaintances but few friends. True friends are willing to expend the energy to be loyal.

A Friend Is Honest

"Better an open reprimand than concealed love. The wounds of a friend are trustworthy, but the kisses of an enemy are excessive" (Prov. 27:5–6). Real friends are honest enough to warn us of dangers we perhaps cannot see. None of us likes to be rebuked, but true friends are willing to risk our displeasure in order to warn us of the consequences of our errors. We often look for ways to flatter people, but we must remember that true friends only give honest compliments.

A Friend Is Committed

Often our attitudes toward other people are characterized by fickleness. Our feelings toward them go up and then down. First we care; then we do not care. But the Bible says, "A friend loves at all times, and a brother is born for a difficult time" (Prov. 17:17). A true friend is consistent and steadfast.

There is a price to pay for friendship: the commitment of time and effort to get to know one another and the commitment of time and effort to protect the relationship. A true friend is a prize and should not be treated lightly.

I am developing a friendship with a Jewish rabbi. He told me a saying the rabbis have: how can you love me when you don't know where I hurt? In other words, we must know where a person hurts and be sensitive to that hurt if we want to cultivate his friendship. Have you spent enough time with your friends to know where they hurt?

Paul said, "I will most gladly spend and be spent for you. If I love you more, am I to be loved less?" (2 Cor. 12:15). He passed the test of commitment. His love for his friends did not make demands, and it stood up under stress.

Larry Walker, my friend since high school, was an all-state basketball player, the president of the senior class, and played first-chair violin in the Albuquerque symphony. He wrote a poem about the principle of commitment, and I would like to share it with you:

How Beautiful Love Is

> My love for you does not depend on how you feel about me.
> I love you enough for both of us.
> True love is not conditioned upon response.
> Reciprocation is not the scale upon which love is balanced.
> My love exists because of you.
> You can hurt me or desert me but nothing will ever change the way I feel.
> And if you should choose to return to me that kind of love,
> How beautiful that would be!

I ask that you love me, not because of what I am.
Love me even in spite of what I am.
True love is not conditioned upon worth.
The object should not determine the degree of love's intensity.
No grounds for narcissistic boasting.
I am not an ornament or a trophy. Yet even the worthlessness can be worthy of love.
And if your love should discover within me one speck that could become of value,
How beautiful that would be!

There was One Who knew His love would be rejected.
Yet He loved anyway.
There was One Who knew the object of His love would be unworthy,
Yet He loved anyway.
Even to the point of giving His very Life to demonstrate that love.
How beautiful love is!

And if the one who rejects would respond. And the one who is unworthy would be transformed.
By the fulfilled life He offers
Through fellowship with Him
How beautiful that would be!

How beautiful that would be![2]

Friends are few and far between. How blessed we are when we have friends like Larry Walker. Cherish your friends. Put the principles of unselfishness, loyalty, honesty, and commitment into practice. Learn from the good things Job's friends did, and also learn from their mistakes.

If you would have friends, then you must be a friend (Prov. 18:24). Jesus told us that it is in giving that we receive (Luke 6:38). We are to be the instruments of God in a hurting world. Our lives are to be lighthouses demonstrating His love and compassion to others—especially to our friends.

Endnotes

1 Author unknown.
2 Used by permission of author.

Chapter 8

Rescue from Despair and Discouragement

Job 22:29

The book of Job contains many statements about God that are untrue. These untrue statements were made by Job's three friends—Eliphaz, Bildad, and Zophar. Job's "wise" counselors attributed his plight to secret sin and said in effect, "If you will just get right with God, you will stop suffering." After Eliphaz and his friends had presented their arguments, the Lord stated His verdict: "I am angry with you and your two friends, for you have not spoken the truth about Me, as My servant Job has" (Job 42:7).

However, the fact that Job's friends missed the point much of the time does not mean that everything they said was wrong. In Job 22:29, for example, Eliphaz spoke a great and important truth that is verified in other portions of scripture. He said, "When others are humiliated and you say, 'Lift them up,' God will save the humble." Four aspects of this true statement merit our consideration: the reality of discouragement; the response to discouragement; reassurance in the face of discouragement; and redemption from discouragement.

Reality of Discouragement

Note that Eliphaz said, "*When* others are humiliated" (italics added), not *if*. Each of us is cast down at one time or another. We are all familiar with the reality of discouragement, loneliness, depression, defeat, failure, and rejection—through personal experience and observation.

One reason we are all cast down is that we have all sinned. Sin separates us from God. When we are cut loose from Him—left to our own resources and limitations—we find that at times life is more than we can bear. We become victims of our circumstances, and we are cast down in the valley of sorrow and discouragement.

As a pastor I received many requests for help from people who were discouraged. Early one week a young minister called to tell me that his wife had just left him. He was devastated and did not know where to turn or what to do. With his life in shambles, his calling and career in disarray, and his chosen bride gone, he was crushed and cast down.

Another morning that same week I arrived at my office about 5:15 AM and noticed that someone had slipped a letter under my door. The letter told the story of the heartaches of a family that was coming apart at the seams. Filled with pain and sorrow, that family was desperate and cast down.

One afternoon that week a deacon at our church called to say that his son had been involved in an automobile accident while returning from a mission trip to Mexico. A drunken driver had crossed the road and caused a head-on collision, injuring his son and killing two others. That deacon was cast down and discouraged.

Another afternoon that week I received the news that the father of one of our church members had died. The bereaved family, who loved their father and were not fully prepared for his death, were deeply saddened and cast down.

And sometimes the tragedies are not always with someone else. Just over a year ago now, my daughter's mother-in-law was shot and killed while answering her door just before Christmas. The killing was intentional; a professional hit man just went to the wrong house. All of us must face the tragedies that threaten our well-being.

The people involved in these situations were going through the valley of discouragement. But they weren't the only ones. The list of hurting, sorrowing, and downcast people is always endless. Their plight is the lot of us all. At one time or another we will all be cast down. Some of us may go through the valley of rejection, or we may face unemployment. Others of us may lose our homes. Drug addiction and alcoholism may victimize our children or our parents. Some of us may suffer physical pain while others may be cast down by slander. Our friends may turn on us, and we may have to walk through the valley of misunderstanding and misrepresentation. Discouragement resulting from one problem or another is the common experience of us all.

The reality is that at this very moment some of us are discouraged, disappointed, and at the end of our rope. Nothing seems to make sense. There seem to be no answers for our confusion. Our hearts cry out, "We can't take any more! We are cast down." Whatever our plans were, they have been foiled. Whatever our dreams were, they have been crushed. What we have dreaded has happened. We are bending, and even breaking, under the pressure and strain of it all.

Response to Discouragement

When we are discouraged we should say, "God will save the humble!" (Job 22:29). This verse speaks directly to people who are discouraged and indirectly to those who are not. It speaks to believers who have victory in their spirits, a sense of the presence of God in their hearts, and His power in their lives. This unique group of people has a distinct outlook and attitude. These people rejoice in what God is doing through their difficulties. Since they can see beyond their present circumstances to the other side of the valley of discouragement, they have the responsibility to encourage those who are cast down and cannot see to the other side of the valley.

This great responsibility has been given to believers by God. We Christians must respond to those who are cast down. The apostle Paul wrote, "Carry one another's burdens; in this way you will fulfill the law of Christ" (Gal. 6:2). Paul was not giving us an option, but a directive. Our heavenly Father wants us to go to those who are discouraged, put our arms around them, and encourage them. We have good news for them: "God will save the humble!" They need to hear the message that God will save the humble person; he need not despair, for God can see him through any difficulty. We must say, "Lift up your heart. There is hope."

Barnabas is an excellent example of a person with an encouraging spirit. His real name was Joses, but the disciples called him Barnabas, "which is translated Son of Encouragement" (Acts 4:36). He was given this nickname because he was always lifting the spirits of those who were cast down and discouraged. Whenever Barnabas appeared, everything seemed a little bit better, and everyone was a little more lighthearted.

Barnabas encouraged Saul of Tarsus when he faced rejection by the Christian community in general and the disciples in particular. The disciples were afraid of him because of his activities before he was converted on the road to Damascus. Saul (later known as Paul) had gone on a mission to Damascus to arrest Christians and bring them back to Jerusalem as captives. He had hated Christians. He had cursed them and threatened them. So the church at Jerusalem was less than enthusiastic about his reported conversion. Luke wrote: "When he arrived in Jerusalem, he tried to associate with the disciples, but they were all afraid of him, since they did not believe he was a disciple. Barnabas, however, took him and brought him to the apostles ..." (Acts 9:26–27). When no one else extended a hand of welcome to Paul, Barnabas—the big-hearted layman with the warm smile—put his arm around Paul's shoulder and encouraged him.

Throughout the book of Acts, we read of Barnabas encouraging people. Luke wrote, for example, about the visit of Barnabas to Antioch, where many had turned to the Lord: "When he arrived and saw the grace of God, he was glad, and he encouraged all of them to remain true to the Lord with a firm resolve of the heart—for he was a good man, full of the Holy Spirit and of faith and large numbers of people were added to the Lord" (Acts 11:23–24).

Acts 11:25 goes on to say, "Then he went to Tarsus to search for Saul." The Christians in Jerusalem had reluctantly accepted Paul, but they were still wary of him and let him go back home to Tarsus in order to get him out of their sight. But when nobody else wanted Paul, Barnabas did. When nobody else trusted Paul, Barnabas believed in him. Barnabas went to Tarsus to encourage Paul to come to Antioch. Acts 11:26 records: "When he had found him he brought him to Antioch. For a whole year they met with the church and taught large numbers ..."

What a tremendous role Barnabas played! It was a bold step to invite the new convert to such a strategic place. Barnabas brought into active ministry a young Christian brother who would move into a much more prominent role than his own. Paul, who wrote nearly half of the New Testament, might have been a dropout if Barnabas had not encouraged him.

"The disciples were first called Christians in Antioch" (Acts 11:26). *Christian*, which means "little Christ," was a term of derision. The enemies of the disciples at Antioch were "accusing" them of being like Jesus. What a compliment to Barnabas's ministry of encouragement!

Barnabas was such an encourager that he was always sharing the truth of the word of God. He shared God's word with believers and with those who were outside the household of faith. For example, the politician Sergius Paulus wanted to hear the word of God, so he sent for Barnabas and Paul (Acts 13:7). Barnabas shared his faith with unbelievers and taught younger believers how to share their faith. He was an encourager who taught others to be encouragers too.

Barnabas was also concerned with the spiritual growth of believers. Referring to those who were committed to the Lord, Acts 13:43 says that Barnabas and Paul "were speaking with them and persuading them to continue in the grace of God." Persuasiveness was characteristic of Barnabas, and he passed on the trait to his protégé, Paul. Oh, how we need gentle and persuasive encouragers in the church today!

Perhaps the most outstanding example of Barnabas's encouragement involved his young nephew, John Mark. John Mark deserted Barnabas and Paul on their first missionary journey. Later the missionaries were planning another mission trip, and Acts 15:37–40 tells us about their conversation:

> Barnabas wanted to take along John Mark. But Paul did not think it appropriate to take along this man who had deserted them in Pamphylia and had not gone on with them to the work. There was such a sharp disagreement that they parted company, and Barnabas took Mark with him and sailed off to Cyprus. Then Paul chose Silas and departed.

Thereafter the book of Acts focuses on Paul and Silas, so we know little about the team of Barnabas and Mark. Nevertheless, we do know that Barnabas rescued Mark for a life of usefulness to God. In fact, John Mark wrote the second gospel! It is in the New Testament, by the grace of God, because Barnabas gave Mark a second chance and encouraged him along the way. The church today needs individuals like Barnabas!

Without the encouragement of Barnabas, the apostle Paul's training would have been incomplete and John Mark would have been lost to effective service. Yet between these two men, fourteen of the twenty-seven books in the New Testament were written. Because Barnabas encouraged them when they were despondent, they were encouraged. "God will save the humble!" That is a promise of God.

Reassurance in the Face of Discouragement

We need to reassure those who are discouraged that God is still able and willing to lift them up and exalt them. Their situation is not hopeless. Help is nearby.

When we are despondent and discouraged, it is easy to feel that God has forsaken us. It is easy to doubt that God really cares. Without reassurance, many of us would fall by the wayside. That is why it is so important for us as Christians to reach out to those who are despairing. We never know how important our reassurance will be to their future ministry. We need to remember that "God will save the humble!"

Anyone who is discouraged is vulnerable to all kinds of sin. Desperation can cause a person to commit immorality, to become dishonest, and to make wild and outrageous claims. Since people are in danger of sinning when they act out of fear or depression or despair, reassurance from us it vital, and we need reassurance ourselves when we are in the valley of discouragement.

How wise my father was when he said, "Son, never make a decision when you are discouraged. The vast majority of the time you will make the wrong one." What a stabilizing impact those words have had on my life and ministry! At one point in my ministry I had a call from a church where I wanted to serve. I loved the town where that church was located, and I was unhappy in the church where I was serving. The more I prayed, however, the more I realized that I was discouraged, so I declined to call. If I had accepted that call, I would have made the wrong decision.

The lonely, the orphan, and the widow are vulnerable, and they need reassurance from us. Many people today feel that no one cares—that no one is interested in them. They are hurting, and they feel isolated and empty. We as God's people must emerge as an army of concerned people who will show them there is hope.

We also need to reassure the doubter. Some people have lost the vitality of their faith. There was a time when their faith was vibrant and alive. The name of Jesus brought a thrill to their hearts. But somewhere along the way they have become indifferent to the things of God. They have not lost their faith, but they have lost their first love.

Normally when something is lost we look for it. We need to help those who have lost the joy of their salvation to look for that joy. We need to tell them there is hope. Jesus taught us to do this through three stories in Luke 15. The lost sheep, the lost coin, and the lost son in those parables were all found. Someone cared enough to pray. Someone cared enough to look.

Some doubters are bogged down in disillusionment with the church and the Christian community. We need to say to them, "There is hope. Don't give up."

There is hope too for those who have fallen into sin. When people fall into sin, the church stands as a reminder that God still loves them. Ironically, today when people sin, church is the last place they want to go. That is a tragedy because forgiveness is what the church is all about. Our Lord said, "Come to Me, all of you who are weary and burdened, and I will give you rest" (Matt. 11:28). Christ Jesus offers hope to the sinner. He welcomes the fallen. God still loves those who have failed, and He offers His forgiveness to them. As His children, we too should offer forgiveness and hope, for there *is* hope in the message of the gospel. The church needs to find those who have fallen and lift them up.

When believers fall, they need forgiveness and restoration. Paul wrote, "Brothers, if someone is caught in any wrongdoing, you who are spiritual should restore such a person with a gentle spirit, watching out for yourselves so you won't be tempted also" (Gal. 6:1). Someone who has fallen needs the attention of a forgiving person who will encourage him to go on with the Lord. The one who is downcast does not need to be surrounded by people who dwell on his mistakes and faults.

Parents give more attention to a sick child than to a healthy child. The parents love both children, but the sick child needs them more. Should the church be any different? Should we spend all our time patting spiritually healthy people on the back and neglect others who do not know the Lord? Should we constantly seek out those who seem to have it all together and avoid those who are hurting? No. We should spend time with those who are hurting. We should be telling those who have fallen into sin about the hope that is found in Christ.

There is also hope for those who grieve. When death intervenes in our lives, we need hope. When divorce breaks our hearts and tears us apart, we need hope. Paul reassured us that comfort is available: "Blessed be the God and Father of our Lord Jesus Christ, the Father of mercies and the God of all comfort" (2 Cor.1:3). Peter reassured us that we will be lifted up: "Humble yourselves therefore under the mighty hand of God, so that He may exalt you in due time, casting all your care upon Him, because He cares about you" (1 Pet. 5:6–7). No matter what pulls us apart or breaks our hearts, there is hope: "Therefore we do not give up; even though our outer person is being destroyed our inner person is being renewed day by day" (2 Cor. 4:16).

When we reassure those who are discouraged, we are sharing the heart of God. When we declare God's lifting power, we are doing God's business and the words of the old hymn come alive:

> Down in the human heart, crushed by the tempter,
> Feelings lie buried that grace can restore;
> Touched by a loving heart, weakened by kindness,
> Cords that are broken will vibrate once more.

> Rescue the perishing,
> Care for the dying;
> Jesus is merciful,
> Jesus will save.[1]

Redemption from Discouragement

When discouragement is the result of sin, redemption is available. First John 1:7 says, "The blood of Jesus Christ His Son cleanses us from all sin." Jesus said, "People will be forgiven every sin and blasphemy ..." (Matt. 12:31). Isaiah 1:18 declares: "'Come now let us discuss this,' says the Lord. 'Though your sins are like scarlet, they will be as white as snow; though they are as red as crimson, they will be like wool.'" These verses of scripture clearly teach that God provides forgiveness for sin. Because Christ took our sins upon Himself, we can become righteous.

The biggest problem you and I have is the very thing that causes us to come to Christ in the first place. We do not come to Him because we are righteous. We come to Him discouraged because we are unrighteous. Our sin causes us to turn to Jesus. When we become aware that there is nothing we have done or that we can do to achieve righteousness, God saves us.

Eliphaz was speaking the truth about God when he said, "He will save the humble (Job 22:29). Our humble confession of sin allows God to forgive our sins and bring us into His family. God does not respond to arrogance. He provides redemption when our hearts turn to Him in humility.

Endnotes

1 From "Rescue the Perishing" by Fanny J. Crosby.

Chapter 9

Man's Inevitable Appointment

Job 30:23

Death is the inevitable experience that we do not like to think about. It has an annoying habit of worming its way into our circle of friends and family, but we pretend that we ourselves will live forever. We act as if death always happens to someone else, never to us, but it is something we cannot avoid. Job faced its grim reality when he said, "I know that You will lead me to death the place appointed for all who live" (Job 30:23).

What Is Death?

According to *Webster's Ninth New Collegiate Dictionary* death is "a permanent cessation of all vital functions: the end of life." This definition is more limited than the teaching about death in the Bible, which speaks of three kinds of death in the human experience: physical death, spiritual death, and eternal death.

In the Bible, death is portrayed as the separation of one part of existence from another part of that existence. Thus death is not the end of life altogether; it is the end of life in one of its expressions. *Physical death* is the separation of the immaterial soul or spirit of an organism from its material body. The immaterial part goes on living in a different expression. For example Luke 16:19–31—the story of Lazarus and the rich man—teaches that life goes on after physical death.

Spiritual death, according to the Bible, is the separation of human beings from God in this life. When Adam disobeyed God in the Garden of Eden, spiritual death entered the human experience. As a result of the fall, every individual is born spiritually dead—sinful by nature, by choice, and by conduct (Rom. 5:12).

Romans 3:23 tells us that "all have sinned and fall short of the glory of God." Thus every person in the world is spiritually dead and must be born again to become spiritually alive (John 3:5–7). The essence of God's work in Christ for the world is to give us spiritual life (John 3:16, 36). Addressing people who had accepted Jesus Christ as their personal Savior, Paul wrote, "You He made alive, who were dead in trespasses and sins" (Eph. 2:1).

Eternal death is the spiritual and physical separation of individuals from God's presence for all eternity. People who experience eternal death are separated from God in this life and in the life to come.

For the one who is apart from God, this life is utter vanity, and judgment is inevitable in the life to come. Ecclesiastes 11:9 says, "Rejoice, young man, while you are young, and let your heart be glad in the days of your youth. And walk in the ways of your heat and in the sights of your eyes; but know that for all of these things God will bring you to judgment." Hebrews 9:27 says, "It is appointed for people to die once and after this, judgment." Acts 17:31 declares, "He has set a day on which He is going to judge the world in righteousness by the Man He has appointed." And Revelation 20:11–12, 15 speaks of that final judgment day, "Then I saw a great white throne and One seated on it. Earth and heaven fled from His presence, and no place was found for them. I also saw the dead, the great and the small, standing before the throne, and books were opened. Another book was opened, which is the book of life, and the dead were judged according to their works by what was written in the books ... And anyone not found written in the book of life was thrown into the lake of fire."

Physical Death

As we think about physical death, we will consider Job 30:23 and the overall teaching of the Bible about man's inevitable appointment.

Job knew that he and "all living" would die. Everyone has been sentenced to death (2 Cor. 1:9)—it is a universal experience. Yet death is intensely personal; each of us has his own appointment.

You and I may have brushed against death and made a thousand escapes; we have avoided that inevitable appointment thus far. But one day each of us will fall into a death snare from which there is no escape. Each of us will keep his appointment.

Because my father died when he was fifty-two years old, I started thinking more about death as I approached my fifty-second birthday. Now death seems more real than it did when I was younger. It seems more personal.

Job's declaration was a statement of absolute certainty: "I *know* that You will lead me to death the place appointed for all who live" (Job 30:23, italics added). It can be intelligently perceived that death is certain. Death is also impartial! It visits young and old, wealthy and poor, single and married, male and female, parent and child, saint and sinner. It is the great equalizer.

I will never forget the first time I was confronted with death. When I was a young minister, I ran to help a woman who had collapsed on the street. I reached down, picked her up, and she died in my arms. It was an eerie experience. One moment there was life; the next moment it was gone. That is the phenomenon we call physical death.

Job said: "Man born of woman is short of days and full of trouble. He blossoms like a flower, then withers; he flees like a shadow and does not last" (Job 14:1–2). The psalmist also spoke of the phenomena of life and death: "For He knows what we are made of, remembering that we are dust. As for man, his days are like grass he blooms like a flower of the field; when the wind passes over it, it vanishes, and its place is no longer known" (Ps. 103:14–16). James 4:14 adds to the description of physical life: "You don't even know what tomorrow will bring what your life will be! For you are a bit of smoke that appears for a little while, then vanishes."

Life is a miracle, but it is fleeting. The phenomenon of death is always impending. Any moment we may pass through the doorway of death. At that point we will be transported from time to eternity—from a sphere bound by the senses to a sphere not bounded by the senses. The transition will be incredible.

The first reference in the Bible to the phenomenon of death is found in Genesis 2:17. Another early reference is found in 2 Samuel 14:14: "For we will certainly die and be like water poured out on the ground, which can't be recovered. But God would not take away a life; He would devise plans so that the one banished from Him does not remain banished." In other words, when we see death we feel helpless; we are not able to renew life. But God is able! He has devised a means for gathering up what has been spilled.

Death is a phenomenon in which the child of God experiences victory. The apostle Paul wrote, "We are confident and satisfied to be out of the body and at home with the Lord" (2 Cor. 5:8). Those who are "out of the body" seem like "water poured out on the ground," but since they are "at home with the Lord" we know they have been "gathered up again." Just as 2 Samuel 14:14 tells us, "He would devise plans so that the one banished from Him does not remain banished," 1 Thessalonians 4:17 tells us, "We will always be with the Lord." When death visits the child of God, the Holy Spirit comes to take his or her spirit to be with the Lord. At the resurrection the bodies of those who know and love God will be gathered up and rejoined to their spirits. In that resurrected state they will live eternally in the presence of the great God and Savior, Jesus Christ.

Job, who looked realistically at the phenomenon of death, knew that he would die at an appointed time. The psalmist understood the same truth. He prayed, "Lord, reveal to me the end of my life and the number of my days. Let me know how transitory I am" (Ps. 39:4). Psalm 90:12 is similar: "Teach us to number our days carefully so that we may develop wisdom in our hearts." James, who was also aware of our appointment with death, taught us to say, "If the Lord wills, we will live and do this or that" (James 4:15).

The imposing precision of death and judgment is clearly and dramatically presented in the New Testament. Hebrews 9:27–28 states: "And just as it is appointed for people to die once and after this, judgment so also the Messiah, having been offered once to bear the sins of many, will appear a second time, not to bear sin, but to bring salvation to those who are waiting for Him." The word "as" in the first clause signals that death—the inevitable appointment of man—can be compared to the inevitable appointment of Christ to die on the cross (John 19:11). Just as surely as Jesus had an appointment on the cross, each of us has an appointment with death. And just as Jesus had His appointment on the cross to reveal God's judgment of sin, the death of each of us is an appointment for judgment.

Acts 1:11 indicates that Jesus has an appointment to come back to earth again. His coming again is as sure as the death of each one of us is sure. We do not know the time of either event, but they are both on God's calendar. God knows when each one of us will die, just as He knows when the trumpet will sound (1 Thess. 4:16) and Jesus will return to establish His Kingdom on earth (Rev. 20:1–6). It is a moment of precision.

God Himself is the source of that precision. Job said, "*You* will lead me to death" (Job 30:23, italics added). Our lives are not like helpless ships on the stormy sea of life. We do not need to be victimized by the turbulence of circumstances. God bears us along with precision from the moment of our birth until the time appointed for our death. We are borne along through life to Himself. That provision takes the pressure off us.

Death is God's prerogative. Psalm 68:20 says, "Escape from death belongs to the Lord God." Ecclesiastes 8:8 says, "No one has authority over the wind to restrain it, and there is no authority over the day of death." Only God has that power. Knowing that the hands of God will bring us to our appointment with death should give us joy and comfort. We can rest in His hands. He will never leave us or forsake us. We are His! He has the power to carry us through the doorway of death into His eternal presence. That means we will not die accidentally. We may die in an accident, but in God's perspective death is never an accident. Before we were even born, God recorded the events of our lives (Ps. 139:15–16). We can make responsible choices that enable God to prolong our lives as it pleases Him, but the time of our death is in God's hands.

The Hour of Death

God's grace, which is sufficient for our day-to-day needs (2 Cor. 12:9), is also sufficient for the hour of death. Many people are greatly concerned and burdened regarding death, but we do not need to worry. Each Christian can say with the psalmist, "Even when I go through the darkest valley, I fear no danger, for You are with me" (Ps. 23:4). Because Paul knew God's grace was sufficient, he could confidently quote the saying: "Death has been swallowed up in victory. O Death, where is your victory? O Death, where is your sting?" (1 Cor. 15:54–55). The apostle could also write, "For me, living is Christ and dying is gain" (Phil. 1:21). Psalm 116:15 assures the believer, "The death of His faithful ones is valuable in the Lord's sight," and Revelation 14:13 says, "Blessed are the dead who die in the Lord from now on."

We live in a day when few people seem to rely on the Lord. Most of us have a "can do" philosophy. We don't like to need or depend on anyone else. Even when facing that inevitable appointment with death, many people place their trust in something other than God.

Some people put their trust in pleasure. They live with gusto and proclaim, "We only go through once!" They do everything that excites and caters to their flesh. They burn the candle at both ends. But what good will the pleasures of this world do for them when they are dying? Paul declared, "She who is self indulgent is dead even while she lives" (1 Tim. 5:6). To live for pleasure is to miss life.

Some people put their trust in knowledge. Now the pursuit of knowledge is commendable, and everyone likes to be regarded as intelligent, but the same thing happens to the wise man as happens to the fool. The fool dies, and so does the wise man. Solomon said: "I realized that there is an advantage to wisdom over folly, like the advantage of light over darkness. The wise man has eyes in his head, but the fool walks in darkness. Yet I also knew that one fate comes to them both" (Eccles. 2:13–14). All the knowledge gained in this life fails at the time of death. (At that point the only advantage the wise man has is a few extra letters on his tombstone: "R.I.P.—PhD"!)

Some people put their trust in material possessions, but to trust in them in vanity. Solomon wrote:

> There is a sickening tragedy I have seen under the sun: wealth kept by its owner to his harm. That wealth was lost in a bad venture, so when he fathered a son, he was empty-handed. As he came from his mother's womb, so he will go again, naked as he came; he will take nothing for his efforts that he can carry in his hands (Eccles. 5:13–15).

Some people put their trust in fame. But famous people as well as obscure people die. What profit is it to celebrities to have their names on all the marquees when it is time to die? What have they gained when their faces are recognized throughout the world? When we reach that appointed time, we all stand on equal footing.

Some people put their trust in their achievements. But Solomon said:

> Thus, I became great and surpassed all who were before me in Jerusalem; my wisdom also remained with me., All that m eyes desired, I did not deny them. I did not refuse myself any pleasure, for I took pleasure in all my struggles. This was my reward for all my struggles. When I considered all that I had accomplished and what I had labored to achieve, I found everything to be futile and a pursuit of the wind. There was nothing to be gained under the sun (Eccles. 2:9–11).

Some people rely on their religion to sustain them when their appointments with death come, but religion will fail too. Solomon concluded that religious formality without commitment is vanity (Eccles. 5:1–7). We can participate in religious observances all our lives and still miss the mark. Unless we know the Lord personally, "We are all like an unclean thing, And all our righteousnesses are like filthy rags" (Isa. 64:6).

What will be our sufficiency at the hour of death? Neither pleasure, nor knowledge, nor material possessions, nor fame, nor achievements, nor religion are trustworthy. We need to take another look at what we are relying on to sustain us through death. Israel had the same need, and Moses said of them, "If only they were wise, they would figure it out; they would understand their fate!" (Deut. 32:29). Like Hezekiah, we need to hear the Lord saying, "Set your house in order, for you shall die, and not live" (2 Kings 20:1). The young, the elderly, the rich, the famous, the wise, the religious—all of us need to consider our fate (our death) and set our houses in order, for we have inevitable appointments with death and judgment. The admonition of Amos 4:12 applies today: "Prepare to meet your God."

Our appointments with death will supersede everything else on our agendas. At its appointed time death will come, perhaps interfering with our plans and dreams. We cannot hold it at bay. And when death comes, we will face eternity. Whatever we trust in this life will determine our eternal experience, so we would be wise to set our spiritual houses in order.

The Fear of Death

Some of us are afraid to die. There are three basic reasons for our fear of death.

First, we may not understand what death is. When we understand what death is, we do not fear it. Faced in the power of the Lord, death is simply a doorway leading into eternity. Death tears down the earthly bodies of believers and ushers them into the presence of the Lord (2 Cor. 5:8). Paul wrote, "We know that if our earthly house, a tent, is destroyed, we have a building from God, a house not made with hands, eternal in the heavens" (2 Cor. 5:1). When we understand death the way Paul did, we are not frightened, we do not "grieve like the rest, who have no hope," and we can "encourage one another" (1 Thess. 4:13, 18).

Second, we may be afraid to meet God, afraid to stand before Him in judgment. This fear is the Holy Spirit's way of telling us we need the Savior. Jesus paid the price for our sins to make us righteous before the Father. We need not be afraid to meet our Father if we know we are clothed in the righteousness of Christ's sinless perfection. Jesus prepared the way so we could enter boldly into God's presence (Heb. 4:16).

Third, we may be ashamed to meet God. Some Christians are afraid to die because they have not lived godly lives. They have accepted Jesus as personal Savior, but they have lied, slandered, gossiped, and committed immorality and been deceitful, hateful, and hypocritical. They have lived in selfishness, pride, and rebellion. If they stood before God today, they would hang their heads in shame. They would want more time so they could set things right.

One of the great tragedies today is that people have lost their ability to be ashamed. They rationalize their sins and justify their actions. Their standards are relativistic. One day, however, they will stand before God and discover that He measures righteousness by an absolute standard. Those who have been ungodly need to turn to Him and ask for forgiveness. Like the centurion of Matthew 8:8, we are all unworthy for the Lord to come under our roofs, but He is always willing to forgive us and to restore us to fellowship (1 John 1:9).

If we are ashamed to meet God, we need to put our houses in order. Satan does not want us to do that, and he will use any ploy to keep us from preparing to meet God. One of his tactics is to use up our time. He tries to trick us into living for tomorrow, and if that does not work, he tempts us to dwell on yesterday. But yesterday is gone and tomorrow has not arrived; the only time we have is today. Satan will do anything to cause us to miss the present.

God is not impressed with our promises or our reminiscences. We must respond now to Jesus, who says: "Listen! I stand at the door the knock. If anyone hears My voice and opens the door, I will come in to him and have dinner with him, and he with Me" (Rev. 3:20).

We do not need to be afraid of death. We can walk in the confidence that God will bring us through death to Himself. We can rest in Him as we pass from this life into the presence of our loving Father. His Son Jesus is the only way through death to God the Father. Jesus said: "I am the way, the truth, and the life. No one comes to the Father except through Me" (John 14:6). Even if you have never accepted the Lord, you can receive Christ as your Savior now and be forgiven and cleansed. If you are not ready to die, will you come to the Father through Him?

Chapter 10

Where in the World Is God?

Job 23:2–4

Lost in a maze of suffering, Job asked in effect, "Where in the world is God?" He could not sense God's presence. Describing his plight, he said, "Today also my complaint is bitter. His hand is heavy despite my groaning" (Job 23:2). Job felt the heavy hand of oppression and cried out: "If only I knew how to find Him, so that I could go to His throne. I would plead my case before Him and fill my mouth with arguments" (Job 23:3–4). Job wanted to plead his case before the Judge and vindicate himself, but how could he argue his case if he couldn't even find the Judge?

At one time or another most of us have asked, "Where in the world is God?" When faced with a difficulty serious enough to prompt the question, we may have sought to solve the problem by moving away or changing our circumstances. Or we may have stood up to the problem—confronting it, struggling with it. These "flight or fight" approaches are seldom the answer. Job did not flee from his difficulties or fight them. He learned to identify them, discern their cause, and discover his options. We can learn some basic principles of problem-solving from Job's experiences.

The Problem

Job's problem was that he felt lost. Desperately needing God but unable to see Him working in his life, Job said, "If I go east, He is not there, and if I go west, I cannot perceive Him" (Job 23:8).

Job felt lost because he could not get away from his suffering. As a friend of mine said when his little girl was in the throes of leukemia, "The constant thing about chronic sickness is that it is constant." Job was experiencing chronic pain and constant suffering. In his agony, he could not see God. He felt all alone, abandoned in his difficulties, and so his complaint was bitter.

The word translated "bitter" in Job 23:2 literally means "rebellious," so Job's use of the word may have suggested to his friends that he was rebellious. Nothing—not even his self-discipline and high resolve—could stop his groaning, and his friends perceived him to be struggling against God.

Some of us have felt personally the kind of pain and emptiness that Job's groaning expressed. Others of us have stood by the bedside of a friend and watched him experience the anguish of intense pain. Watching helplessly as a loved one slipped into the final stage of cancer, we have changed our prayer from, "Lord, please give this dear one back to me" to, "Lord, please take your servant home."

When we seek the face of God for our suffering loved ones and the suffering does not end, we draw close to the cry of Job: "If only I knew how to find Him" (Job 23:3). This universal lament comes from the heart of everyone who suffers and everyone whose loved ones suffer. When our pain is unbearable, we feel separated from God. The heavy hand of suffering obliterates our sense of His presence.

Job also felt lost because he was confused. Neither he nor his friends understood why he was suffering. The explanations they offered were theologically wrong and confused Job even more. They told Job he was suffering because he was sinful; if he were right with God, he would not be suffering. Job's friends meant well, but they did not have the right solution. In his confusion, Job's heart cried out for an answer.

Many of us do not have the physical pain Job had, but we can identify with his confusion. The theological errors that abound today in the explanations people offer for physical, emotional, and spiritual suffering are astounding. Mr. Smith tells us one reason for our difficulties, and Mrs. Jones tells us the opposite. If we aren't careful and spiritually discerning, we could become theologically schizophrenic. We could find ourselves moving off into some doctrinal never-never land instead of obtaining correct perspectives on the world in which we live. We could also become confused if we try to reason things through for ourselves without a firm grasp of the teachings of God's word.

Sometimes it is hard to know what the right answer is. Our opinions change from day to day. Confusion enters our lives, and we become choice targets for Satan and his forces. Satan's primary objective is to turn us away from God and if he cannot do this, to keep us confused. When we become confused about what is right, about what is truth, or about what God's word says, we feel lost and separated from God. That is why our faith in God needs to be simple and direct. We need to trust God, believe His word, and allow Him to instruct us and build us up in the faith.

Finally, *Job felt lost because he was isolated and alone.* Job was the best-known man in his community. He had a large family and lots of friends, but when tragedy struck he lost his family and most of his friends. The few remaining friends accused him of secret sin, and even his wife scorned him. Job was ruined, and he was alone. He could not even sense the presence of God.

We feel isolated with God when there is a breach in our fellowship with God's people. We cannot be right with God and wrong with our fellow man. That is why the New Testament gives a clear edict that Christians are to be reconciled to one another (John 13:34–35; Eph. 4:32; 1 John 2:8–10; 4:7). Whenever we are in conflict with other believers, we experience loneliness and feel alienated from God.

Job could not sense the presence of God, but he longed to be able to. He remembered what it was like to walk and talk with God, and he longed to experience that fellowship.

God often spoke to individuals directly during the patriarchal period of the Old Testament. Because the Torah had not yet been written, Job obviously had received his carefully developed theology directly from God. He argued with his three friends on the basis of truth he had learned from the mouth of God. So Job knew what it was like a commune with God, and he yearned to recapture the sense of His presence.

Once we have walked in close fellowship with God and have heard His voice speak to our hearts, we want to have that relationship sustained. If we have known the joy of hearing God's call and felt the warmth of the Holy Spirit flooding our souls, we long to experience that joy and warmth again. If there ever was a time in our lives when God's presence was more real than the breath we drew, we yearn to sense His presence again.

Job had experienced God's presence in the past, and he longed to meet God again. The statements of his friends, however, did not reflect that same longing. Job wanted another encounter with God, but his friends did not seem to have the same desire. Job's longing can be distinguished from his friends' in that it was personal and passionate. These two essentials must characterize our longing if we are to experience God's presence in our own lives.

It is imperative that our longing be *personal*. The pronoun "I" or "my" is used six times in Job 23:2–4. Job was seeking God's presence by reaching out to Him personally, and if we are to experience God's presence, we must personally pursue Him with our hearts. Our longing must be as personal as the psalmist's: "As a deer longs for streams of water, so I long for You, God. I thirst for God, the living God. When can I come and appear before God?" (Ps. 42:1–2).

Many times we pray editorially, saying, "Lord, *we* pray …" This may sound polite, but it is also impersonal. When we are vitally related to God, we do not need to stand on ceremony. Job's quest was so personal that he spoke as if no one else existed besides him and God. If our hearts yearn for Him, we will cry, "Regardless of whoever else wants to know or whoever else is searching, I want to know. I am searching." We will say with the apostle Paul: "But everything that was a gain to me, I have considered to be a loss because of Christ. More than that, I also consider everything to be a loss in view of the surpassing value of knowing Christ Jesus my Lord. Because of Him I have suffered the loss of all things and consider them filth, so that I may gain Christ" (Phil. 3:7–8).

Our longing for a sense of the presence of God must be *passionate* as well as personal. Job searched with intensity, and his prayers were fervent. His desire to find God was all-consuming. Job had a heart akin to Simon Peter's, for when Jesus asked the disciples if they would turn away from Him, Peter said, "Lord, who will we go to? You have the words of eternal life" (John 6:68).

In contrast to Job, many of us search for God's presence casually. Often we daydream in worship services, and our prayers lack intensity. Our passion is focused on something other than God. We are intent on what *we* want, and we are wrapped up in what *we* think. We will never have a desire as strong as Job's if our minds are misdirected.

If we think the solution to our problems is to have more money in the bank, we will never long for God's presence with the passion of Job. If we think, consciously or subconsciously, that anything in this world can satisfy us, we will turn our attention away from God. When David thought he could find fulfillment with Bathsheba, he disregarded the Lord. When we push God aside, we are in serious danger; we have placed an idol between ourselves and the Lord.

Job realized that all the possessions, influence, and friends he had had could not give him the satisfaction he desired. Job never prayed to be restored; he prayed to find God. After acknowledging his sin, David prayed the same way: "God, create a clean heart for me and renew a steadfast spirit within me. Do not banish me from Your presence or take Your Holy Spirit from me. Restore the joy of Your salvation to me, and give me a willing spirit" (Ps. 51:10–12).

Likewise, many of us need to repent. Instead of turning toward God as a last resort or when we feel that He will help us get what we want, we should passionately long for Him the way Job and David did. Otherwise we will not experience His presence.

The Solution

We have identified Job's problem: he felt lost, and he longed for a sense of the presence of God. We have also discerned the causes of his problem: he could not get away from his suffering; he was confused; and he felt isolated and alone. In considering his options, he realized that his friends did not have the right solution.

When we feel lost, what options do we have? We have already discovered that in order to sense the presence of God, our longing for the experience must be as personal and passionate as Job's. Having come to the knowledge that this world cannot satisfy the desires of our hearts, we must repent of our wandering away from God. But there are also practical steps we can take as we turn our attention back to the Lord.

The surest way to find God's presence in our lives is to *search the word of God daily*. We can get to know God by getting to know what He has said to His people through His written word. The Bible is God's revelation of Himself and His will for us. Instead of just reading what others have written about the Bible, we should become personally familiar with God's word. As we do, we will rely less on what people say about the Bible and more on what the Bible says about people. As Psalm 119:9 says, "How can a young man keep his way pure? By keeping Your word."

We don't have to understand the entire Bible in order to apply its truths. Even the simplest mind can understand enough to acquire knowledge of God and what He says about life. That is why the psalmist wrote, "I have treasured Your word in my heart so that I may not sin against You. Lord, may You be praised; teach me Your statues" (Ps. 119:11–12).

Another practical step to finding a sense of God's presence is to *join with other Christians in worship*. Hebrews 10:25 says, "Not staying away from our meetings, as some habitually do, but encouraging each other, and all the more as you see the day drawing near." We need fellowship with one another. Remember, loneliness is one of the reasons people do not sense God's presence. As God's children, we draw strength from each other. Many times God uses someone's encouraging words or actions to meet our needs or to guide us in a direction He wants us to follow. When our circumstances cause us to feel that we are far from God, the best place for us to be is with His people. Worshiping together is a part of God's masterful plan for knitting us together into whole people. As the apostle Paul put it:

> So then you are no longer foreigners and strangers, but fellow citizens with the saints, and members of God's household, built on the foundation of the apostles and prophets, with Christ Jesus Himself as the cornerstone. The whole building is being fitted together in Him and is growing into a holy sanctuary in the Lord, in whom you also are being built together for God's dwelling in the Spirit (Eph. 2:19–22).

To *obey* God is one more practical step in the search for the presence of God. Have you ever observed that when children are disobedient, they avoid their parents? Likewise when we are knowingly disobedient to God's will, we push Him away. God may seem distant to us because we have pushed Him away. So if we are wondering, "Where in the world is God?" we should check our activities to see if we are doing something that God has forbidden. The best way to stay close to God is to obey Him.

Although Job felt *lost* and he was *longing* for God's presence, he was actually *living* in God's presence. Even when Job was not able to sense God's presence, he knew that God was there. Notice how he expressed that truth: "When He is at work to the north, I cannot see Him; when He turns south, I cannot find Him" (Job 23:9). Job knew God was working in his life, but he felt that God was purposely hiding Himself. Living through these trying times when he could not see God was an exercise of faith for Job.

Job's words in 23:9 also reveal that we can never find God through our own effort. We never will see God just through human eyes. Many people claim that they see God in nature, but they don't. What they see are evidences of God. Psalm 19:1 testifies, "The heavens declare the glory of God, and the sky proclaims the work of His hands." If we don't see God through eyes of faith, we never will see Him.

We do not find God as a result of our reasoning. We find God when we discover Him through Jesus Christ. Jesus said, "I am the way, the truth, and the life. No one comes to the Father except through Me" (John 14:6). Philip said, "Lord, show us the Father, and that's enough for us," and Jesus responded, "The one who has seen Me has seen the Father" (John 14:8–9). Through the eyes of faith we see God in Jesus.

Job 11:7–9 records a legitimate question and the answer: "Can you fathom the depths of God or discover the limits of the Almighty? They are higher than the heavens what can you do? They are deeper than Sheol what can you know? Their measure is longer than the earth and wider than the sea." In other words, we cannot find God merely by searching for Him. God's truth is not irrational, but it cannot be found solely through rational activity. We know from the New Testament that we find God through Jesus. Rational evidence merely supports what we have already accepted by faith.

Job found God through faith in the promise of a Redeemer. Without changing his circumstances, he went from feeling separated from God's presence to knowing that God was with him. "He knows the way that I have taken," he said. "When He has tested me, I will emerge as pure gold" (Job 23:10). Suddenly Job's eyes of faith were opened, and he realized that God was testing him. Although he still did not understanding everything about the test, he realized that God was present in his experiences. That realization changed Job's perspective.

We too sometimes ask, "Where in the world is God?" In the midst of economic crises, broken relationships, bereavement, disappointments, and despair we turn to find God and wonder where He is. When we cannot see God, we need to remember that He is right there looking out for us. He is always present in our experiences, and He is always working in our lives for our benefit. "We know that all things work together for the good of those who love God: those who are called according to His purpose" (Rom. 8:28). Even when we cannot find a logical explanation for our circumstances, we see through the eyes of faith that God is still guiding us. Job moved by faith to an awareness of God's presence, and by faith we too can enjoy the assurance of God's presence in our lives.

Chapter 11

After Death, What?

Job 14:14; 19:25-27

The book of Job, one of the oldest in the Old Testament, relates events that occurred in the time frame of the Hebrew patriarchs: Abraham, Isaac, and Jacob. This time frame is reflected in the age of the main character (Job 42:16), in the way Job's wealth was calculated, and in his role as family priest. The invasions of the Sabeans and the Chaldeans also help to date the book.

Given the time frame, we would expect Job to have only a primitive understanding of God. We are astonished at how much God revealed to Job and his contemporaries. (God does not always do things the way we would expect!) As we look at that revelation from our side of the resurrection, we discover truth that is meaningful to us today.

When Job asked why he was experiencing the calamities that had befallen him and his family, God rolled back the curtain of revelation and gave him a glimpse of something exciting. In a day when life after death was scarcely understood, God gave Job a glimpse of the truth of the resurrection of the body. Job's understanding of what he saw was limited, but from this side of Calvary we can see an eternity of significance in God's revelation to Job.

Job exclaimed, "But I know my living Redeemer, and He will stand on the dust at last. Even after my skin has been destroyed, yet I will see God in my flesh. I will see Him myself; my eyes will look at Him, and not as a stranger. My heart longs within me" (Job 19:25–27). Job knew that he had a Redeemer who would vindicate him and set the record straight. Knowing that his words were inspired by God, Job said, "I wish that my words were written down, that they were recorded on a scroll or were inscribed in stone forever by an iron stylus and lead!" (Job 19:23–24). Job would have liked to have his words engraved on his tombstone so that people who visited his grave would know that he had died with the hope of the resurrection. But God did better than that. He inscribed Job's words in scripture. Thousands of years later we can read of Job's belief in the resurrection.

At the end of his ordeal Job looked back on the revelation God had given him and said, "Surely I spoke about things I did not understand, things too wonderful for me to know" (Job 42:3). Although Job did not completely comprehend the revelation, it filled him with hope. In order to understand the basis for Job's belief in a life after death, we need to consider two passages from scripture: Job 14:14 and Job 19:25–27.

Job 14:14

First we confront a question. Job asked, "When a man dies, will he come back to life?" (Job 14:14). The condition is certain, not speculative; Job accepted the reality of death. His body was racked with pain, and he thought he was about to die. Agonizing over the mystery and inevitability of death, Job was asking, "Will *I* live again?"

Sad to say, many people today do not ask that question. They live, eat, drink, seek to make their hearts glad, and occupy their time with trivialities but never give serious consideration to what happens after a man dies. Scrambling after preoccupations, many never stop to ask, "What is life? After I die, what then?" Job, on the other hand, faced the reality of death and asked, "Will I live again?"

On the surface Job's question appears to be an inquiry about whether a man can come back to life. What Job really asked was something quite different. He was actually asking, "If a man dies physically, is he still alive?" In other words, "Do I stop living when I die?" It was a question about the immorality of the soul—about the immorality of the real you and the real me. Will we continue to live after our physical bodies die?

We human beings are instilled with a desire for perfection and completion, but even a casual look at life suggests that we never reach perfection or completion during our brief time on earth. We sense that there has to be something more—something beyond this short span of existence—if we are to realize all our potential. Even the greatest philosophers of Greece spoke about the mortality of the soul. They could not deny either.

Physical life is a magnificent miracle, but it is impossible to measure the circumference of our lives by the few days of our earthly sojourn. The real meaning of life lies somewhere beyond this mortal existence. Seeing the futility, frustration, and disappointment of his present circumstances, Job wanted to know about the real meaning of life. That is why he asked, "When a man dies, is he still alive?"

In the New Testament, Jesus answered yes to Job's question. He said: "I am the resurrection and the life. The one who believes in Me, even if he dies, will live. Everyone who lives and believes in Me will never die ever" (John 11:25–26). The Bible clearly states that when a person dies physically, he or she is still alive spiritually. A place has been prepared for us to live when we die. We will live either in God's heaven or in the place prepared for those who reject God and His Son.

Before we can experience life after death, we are required to complete all our days of our "struggle" (Job 14:14). The pattern for our lives on earth is "struggle." We can be thankful that our present state is not an eternity. The confusion and difficulty in which we find ourselves today will not last forever. Although these days of conflict and disappointment may seem long, they will end. The darkness that overwhelms us now will someday succumb to the light at the end of our days of "struggle." The apostle Paul said; "The sufferings of this present time are not worth comparing with the glory that is going to be revealed to us" (Rom. 8:18). Sometimes life seems too sorrowful and stressful to bear, but the time will come when burdens will be lifted.

The Hebrew expression translated "struggle" sometimes implies military service. In Isaiah 40:2 "struggle" was used in reference to the Babylonian exile. In Job 14:14 the King James translators rendered the expression "appointed time," perhaps because the original word suggested a specific time of service. Like the end of a military tour of duty or a period of captivity, our "struggle" will be completed at an appointed time. Throughout the Bible death is spoken of as an appointed time (see Heb. 9:27).

Job spoke of his "appointed time" as "the *days* of my struggle" (italics added). Like him, we need to live life one day at a time. We could not handle life if God gave it to us in big chunks. We may not have the grace to take care of a whole week at a time, but we can take care of one day at a time. God gives us the grace we need—as we need it. Satan tries to get us to dwell on the past or the future so that we'll miss today, but today is the only day we have. And all our days of "struggle" are strategic in that they make up the only period of time that God gives us.

Job said, "All the days of my *struggle until my relief comes*" (Job 14:14, italics added). In this statement he reached out longingly to the prospect of life after death. Life on earth is a struggle, but there is a promise associated with that struggle for the individual who places his trust in God. The struggle will be followed by a change.

The picture suggested is of a group of battle-weary soldiers being replaced by a group of fresh soldiers. Relief is coming to the child of

God who is worn out from fighting. Life is harsh, but there is hope. In effect Job was telling himself, "Help is on the way. Relief is coming."

The relief Job expected is even greater than he understood it to be. What the Holy Spirit revealed to Job in part, we now understand more fully. Darkness will change to light. Difficulty will change to ease. Time will change to eternity. Bitterness will change to sweetness. Fear will change to hope. Our wandering will be over, and we will find our way home. Our weakness will be replaced by strength. Our tears will become rainbows, and our laments will become songs of praise to the Lord, our Redeemer.

Job 19:25–27

The word *Redeemer* occurs twenty-nine times in the Old Testament, perhaps most graphically in the book of Ruth. There we read of the family redeemer, Boaz. In ancient Israel a family (or kinsman) redeemer was responsible for protecting the interests of his extended family. He was to redeem a relative who had sold himself into slavery (Lev. 25:47–49), redeem the land that a poor relative had sold outside the family (Lev. 25:25–28), avenge the killing of a relative (Num. 35:19–21), and provide an heir for a brother who had died (Deut. 25:5–10). Abraham also acted as a family redeemer when he pursued the kings who had taken his nephew Lot captive (Gen. 14). Abraham vindicated, defended, and took up the cause of a kinsman to bring about truth and justice.

Job introduced his Redeemer as One he knew personally: "I know my Living Redeemer" (Job 19:25). Job had personal knowledge of the truth that his Redeemer would never die. The word "lives" is emphatic. Job spoke of a Redeemer who is alive right now and will always be alive. Although Job thought his own death was imminent, he knew that his Redeemer would live to take up his cause and vindicate him of his friends' false charges.

Job had a true Friend in the midst of his false friends. He had a true Comforter in the midst of his miserable comforters. His Redeemer was and is alive. Job was estranged from his earthly friends, but he had a true Friend who would always be there. Like the hymn writer, Job could say with confidence:

> Just when I need Him most,
> Just when I need Him most,
> Jesus is near, to comfort and cheer,
> Just when I need Him most.
> —William C. Poole

Our Lord and Savior Jesus Christ will take care of false charges made against us. But what about the valid charges? We are all sinners. Romans 3:23 says, "All have sinned and fall short of the glory of God." Isaiah 53:6 says, "We all went astray like sheep; we all have turned to our own way." But 1 John 2:1–2 says, "If anyone does sin, we have an advocate with the Father Jesus Christ the righteous One. He Himself is the propitiation for our sins, and not only for ours, but also for those of the whole world." Our Redeemer will take care of the legitimate charges against us.

How can Jesus be our Advocate? How can He take our iniquity upon Himself? He can do so because He is God's Son, who came into the world to redeem us from our sin. Jesus told His disciples that He must suffer, die, and be raised again, and Paul wrote, "Christ died for our sins according to the scriptures, that He was buried, that He was raised on the third day according to the scriptures" (1 Cor. 15:3–4).

When Jesus completed His atoning work on the cross, He said, "It is finished!" (John 19:30). Those three English words are the translation of one Greek word, *tetelestai*. Since *tetelestai* is in the perfect tense, we know that Jesus Christ's substitutionary work on our behalf has been completed and the results abide. How glorious that is for us.

Romans 10:9 says, "If you confess with your mouth, 'Jesus is Lord,' and believe in your heart that God raised Him from the dead, you will be saved." The bodily resurrection of Jesus Christ is the heart of the gospel, for it is our risen and living Lord who intercedes for us before the throne of grace. It is the risen Lord who is our eternally living Redeemer.

Job 19:25 says of our Redeemer that "He will stand on the dust *at last*" (italics added). What this means for us is that God will have the last word. It may seem as if Satan has won the day in our individual struggle against him. Satan certainly appeared to be the winner when Job was afflicted and when Jesus was led to the cross. Our Lord's disciples must have felt terribly defeated as they heard the roll of those Roman drums. Their hopes and dreams were crushed. But the last word had not been spoken. The final words were, "It is finished." The results abide. Then on the morning of the third day Jesus came out of the tomb alive! As John the Baptist said, "Here is the Lamb of God, who takes away the sin of the world!" (John 1:29). God, in the person of His dear Son, Jesus Christ, will render the final verdict.

Job 19:25 says that our Redeemer "will *stand* on the dust at last" (italics added). What a beautiful picture of our Redeemer and King. The posture of standing is significant. Standing indicates that our Redeemer is not the victim; He is the victor! He is not the conquered; He is the conqueror! Our Redeemer stands victorious over sin and death.

Job's spiritual journey reached its climax in 19:25. Every time he became discouraged, he returned to this point of reference. In his heart he kept coming back to his personal experience in knowing that his Redeemer lives and knowing that He will stand victoriously upon the earth. Job knew he might not be vindicated here, but he knew that his Redeemer would vindicate him at last. That same knowledge can be ours if the Lord Jesus Christ is our personal Savior.

After referring to Christ's resurrection, Job presented a picture of our resurrection: "Even after my skin has been destroyed, yet I will see God in my flesh. I will see Him myself; my eyes will look at Him, and not as a stranger" (Job 19:26–27). Death will destroy our bodies, but we will still be alive, and we will see God. What a glorious prospect for everyone who knows Jesus Christ as his personal Savior! We will see God face to face.

Job was so certain he would see God that he repeated the thought. The word "see" in 19:26 and 27 are translations of the Hebrew word meaning "to behold as in a vision, to behold by supernatural revelation." Job experienced a supernatural vision of future events. In the light of New Testament truth we can understand the revelation more fully than he could, and we are reassured by the words of 1 John 3:2: "Dear friends, we are God's children now, and what we will be has not yet been revealed. We know that when He appears, we will be like Him, because we will see Him as He is."

Notice that Job did not say, "I will see the saints." He did not say, "I will see my family." Job said, "I will see God in my flesh." There is no doubt that he would see the saints, but they were not significant in 19:26. Job spoke as if God were the sum and substance of heaven, and He is! Revelation 22:5 says, "Night will no longer exist, and people will not need lamplight or sunlight, because the Lord God will give them light."

After describing the revelation of his resurrection, Job added, "My heart longs within me!" (Job 19:27). The statement has also been translated, "Though my heart faint within me." This alternate translation gives the impression that Job was so overwhelmed by his divine encounter that he was exhausted as well as exhilarated. The thought that he whose life was collapsing around him would see God face to face was overwhelming. Oh, that we might encounter God in such a way that we would be exhilarated and exhausted!

What Job saw darkly, we now see clearly. The resurrection of Jesus Christ is the fulfillment of what Job saw. The King who was coming to redeem the world has arrived, and He has completed His work of redemption. The hope of eternity is revealed in Him. Jesus Christ is the

One who brings meaning to our struggles and trials. He brings comfort, courage, and forgiveness. Today He is entering the hearts of those who will receive Him, and someday He will return in glory to give humanity a new heaven and a new earth. Then we will stand before Him in awe and reverence.

Chapter 12

When God Steps Down

Job 40:1–14

The book of Job consists of a series of dialogues: first between the Lord and Satan, then between Job and his friends, and finally between the Lord and Job. During the time Job was quarreling and debating with his friends, he was longing for God to appear and vindicate him. At last the Lord spoke to Job out of the whirlwind. There is no particular significance to the Lord's speaking out of the whirlwind. The important point is not *how* He spoke, but *that* He spoke.

God is not limited in how He can speak to us. Hebrews 1:1–2 says, "Long ago God spoke to the fathers by the prophets at different times and in different ways. In these last days, He has spoken to us by His Son, whom He has appointed heir of all things and through whom He made the universe." God used many different methods of speaking to His people in Bible times, and He seldom used the same method twice. The Lord spoke to Jacob in a dream (Gen. 28:10–17), to Moses through a burning bush (Exod. 3:1–4:17), and to Elijah in a still, small voice (1 Kgs. 19:9–18). The Lord spoke to Isaiah from His throne (Isa. 6) and to Zacharias and Mary through the angel Gabriel (Luke 1:5–38).

The Lord spoke to Saul (Paul) on the road to Damascus (Acts 9:1–9) and revealed Jesus Christ to John while he was in exile on Patmos (Rev. 1:9—3:22).

Up to the time God spoke out of the whirlwind, Job had been asking all the questions. Now it was the Lord's turn to ask Job some questions. In this encounter (Job 38–41) the Lord asked more than seventy difficult questions on a wide range of subjects, and Job was unable to answer a single one. It is significant that the Lord never answered Job's questions. He did not respond to ethical or theological issues in this dialogue, since Job's questions were basically relational. Job did not need understanding; he needed to learn to trust the Lord.

Job Contended with the Lord

Ludicrously acting as if God were subject to him, Job had tried to put God on the witness stand. Now the tables were turned, and God put Job on the witness stand: "Will the One who contends with the Almighty correct Him? Let him who argues with God give an answer ... Get ready to answer Me like a man; When I question you, you will inform Me" (Job 40:2, 7).

Using questions, the Lord then showed Job's foolishness in complaining to Him. "Do you have an arm like God's? Can you thunder with a voice like His? ... Look at Behemoth, which I made along with you ..." (Job 40:9, 15). Job was not present when God created the universe and he knew nothing about God's reasons for any of His actions. Job's complaints had been misdirected, inappropriate, and impertinent.

Job had been trying to correct God. The word "correct" in Job 40:2 is a translation of a Hebrew word meaning "to admonish or instruct." Job wanted God to act differently—to do things the way he would do them. Job had been saying that if God knew what was going on, things would be different. If God were truly fair, He would not have allowed him to experience his calamities. Job's bottom line had been that God is not righteous. In contending with God, he was treading on dangerous ground.

The great struggle in theology and intellectual pursuits in the Christian world today centers around the same issue: Are we going to let God be God, or are we going to play God? Are we going to acknowledge Him, or are we going to correct Him? We should be very cautious about correcting someone's work unless we have something better to put in its place.

History is filled with accounts of men who criticized or condemned God and other people in order to bolster their high opinions of themselves. In the Garden of Eden, Satan questioned the integrity and character of God and tempted Adam and Eve by promising them that they would be as wise as God (Gen. 3:1–5). That is how original sin began.

Some of us feel good when we criticize others, and we may even try to bolster our egos by criticizing God. Like Job, we may be concerned that God has let things get out of hand. We may feel that God does not realize what is happening in our circumstances, that He does not understand all the pain and heartache we are experiencing. When we feel that way, we are arguing or contending with God. We are questioning His character and integrity.

Job Confessed to the Lord

When the Lord challenged Job, he answered, "I am so insignificant. How can I answer You? I place my hand over my mouth. I have spoken once, and I will not reply; twice, but now I can add nothing" (Job 40:4–5). Job was not saying he was a terrible sinner. He was acknowledging that he was insignificant in comparison to God.

During the debates with his friends, Job had longed to hear God speak, but when God actually did speak, Job was overwhelmed and awestruck. He exclaimed in effect, "I am nothing! I am speechless. I will say nothing else." Job's words remind us of Isaiah's words when he saw the Lord high and lifted up: "Woe is me, for I am ruined, because I am a man of unclean lips and live among a people of unclean lips, and because my eyes have seen the King the Lord of Hosts" (Isa. 6:5).

Since we tend to cower and remain silent out of respect for someone very important, we might expect the Lord to have wanted Job to remain silent. But the Lord did not want Job to remain silent. God said, "When I question you, you will inform Me" (Job 40:7). The Lord did not want Job's silence. He wanted Job's heart. He wanted all of Job. God also wants all of us.

God Responded to Job

God does not condemn our questions and our doubts. In fact, the Lord vindicated Job, who had asked all the questions, and condemned his three friends who had tried to provide all the answers (Job 42:7).

God is not afraid of our questions. He does not expect us to go through life without asking questions or expressing doubts. The issue is not whether we will ever have questions or doubts, but what we will do when we have them. We learn from the example of Job to bring our questions and our doubts to God. God will deal with them. We learn the same lesson from James 1:5: "If any of you lacks wisdom, he should ask God, who gives to all generously and without criticizing, and it will be given to him." Do not be afraid to bring your doubts and questions to God.

When Job confessed his inadequacies, something interesting happened. In essence the Lord said:

> I am going to step down, Job. I want you to imagine that you are God, and I want you to tell Me how you would handle things better than I have handled them. For the sake of argument, you are in control of the universe. I want you to see if you can administer it better than I have administered it.

Remember, there are some things you must do. First you must flex your muscles. Do you have an arm like Mine? Next you must speak with authority. Do you have a voice like Mine? Now you must dress yourself with majesty and splendor, and array yourself with glory and beauty. How do you like that? Does your majesty, splendor, glory, and beauty compare with Mine? You have been so critical of Me for the way I have handled things, so now you be God.

God let Job have the heady feeling of power and authority. He challenged him to imagine that he was God and to compare himself with the Almighty. And when Job compared his righteousness with the righteousness of God, he found himself wanting. Isaiah 64:6 speaks of how we all compare with God; "All of us have become like something unclean, and all our righteous acts are like a polluted garment." And Paul said, "All have sinned and fall short of the glory of God" (Rom. 3:23).

We cannot even imagine what it is like to be God. We cannot imagine being arrayed in majesty and splendor, glory and beauty; being strong enough to hold the whole universe in the palm of one hand; having a voice that can be heard anywhere in the universe. It takes the whole universe to inscribe the description of God, so we can only sing:

> Oh Lord my God, when I in awesome wonder
> Consider all the worlds Thy hands have made,
> I see the stars, I hear the rolling thunder,
> Thy pow'r thro'out the universe displayed.
>
> Then sings my soul, My Savior God, to Thee;
> How great Thou art, how great Thou art![1]

Job could not imagine being like God any more than we can, but the conversation between the Lord and Job continued. God said to him: "Unleash your raging anger; look on every proud person and humiliate him. Look on every proud person and humble him; trample the wicked where they stand" (Job 40:11–12). We could paraphrase this verse to read, "Job, when I step down and you imagine yourself to be God, your first assignment will be to look on everyone who is proud and bring him low. You think the wicked should all be brought down. Well, go and do it!" In effect the Lord was saying to Job: "You are questioning how I am handling things, but if you are unable to imagine how I do My work in the first place, how can you know I am not doing it well? Who are you to judge whether I am doing things right?"

We cannot comprehend all the responsibilities God has, and we cannot imagine how He attends to all the details involved. How can He hear the cry of a child in New Delhi and the cry of another child in New Orleans at the same time? How does God know exactly where they live, exactly what they need, and exactly what they want? If we cannot imagine how His administration works, how can we tell Him He is not handling things right? How could Job—afflicted though he was—accuse God of not doing well? That is the question the Lord put before Job.

Our minds are not big enough, quick enough, or trained enough to imagine how God can work all things together for good. But that is God's problem, not ours. We believe His promise and say with Paul, "We know that all things work together for the good of those who love God: those who are called according to His purpose" (Rom. 8:28). Things may not work together in ways we can understand, but God will work all things together for our ultimate good.

Job's questions are not answered specifically because the answers lie in a realm where human wisdom cannot follow. If we expect to solve the problems raised in the book of Job with our limited human understanding, we are wasting our time. Job did not get specific answers, but he discovered the elementary truth that he was not God! We, like Job, need to be reminded of that truth periodically. Only God is capable of being God!

Every human criticism of God presumes that man knows as much as God knows, that man is God's equal. Thus every criticism of God is a form of idolatry. Someone or something is being set up as the equivalent of God. Twenty-first century Americans who think that God should have arranged the world so that we could be more comfortable have made a god out of their own comfort.

The most radiant Christians I have met do not live in the United States. They do not live in the same comfort zone of luxury that many of us know. Grateful for the way the Lord is working His grace in their lives, they cry out with thanksgiving for all that God has done and is doing for them. They cannot afford the "luxury" of such habits as criticism, contentiousness, pettiness, complaining, or backbiting.

We Respond to God

Whenever we find ourselves becoming critical or contentious, we can be sure that we are moving away from God. If we were in fellowship with God, such behavior would break our hearts because it breaks His heart. Critical or contentious attitudes should drive us to our knees in prayer in order to ask God to correct us.

When we think that God should have made us more comfortable than we are, we imply—as Job did—that God has missed the mark. When we think that God's best for us is a sunny day, perfect relationships with other people, and enough responsibility to challenge us, but not so much that it overwhelms us, we imply that we know how God should carry out His responsibilities toward us. But we must remember that our thoughts are based on the inappropriate assumption that when we have everything we want, we are experiencing God's work in our lives.

We like to think that God's purposes are achieved in the sunshine, but after walking with Job through his experiences, we see that God's purposes may be achieved in the valley of the shadow of death. We need to find the focal point of Christian faith in the cross, not the crown.

When we look to Calvary—that horrible, monstrous, and bleak place of tragedy according to our human standards—we will find that the Lord is present. We will be able to say with Paul, "I no longer live, but Christ lives in me. The life I now live in the flesh, I live by faith in the Son of God, who loved me and gave Himself for me" (Gal. 2:20). In the cross we discover that what seems to be the ultimate denial of divine sovereignty is the place where the power of God provides salvation. The cross of Jesus Christ is a place of mystery, but it holds the key to heavenly light.

The book of Job teaches us that God is always at work in our lives. Sometimes He works in the sunshine. Sometimes He works in the shadows. Either way God is always fully present in all His power. We should never measure the value of God's work in our lives by our circumstances. Our conclusions may be based on faulty premises. The worth of God's work is not determined by how we rate it. We can never be God, nor can we ever correct Him. The Lord says, "For My thoughts are not your thoughts, and your ways are not My ways" (Isa. 55:8).

In the end Job understood that God does not allow the wicked to prosper because He is indulgent or weak. Rather, He chooses not to destroy the wicked because of His genuine love for His creation. What appears to be God's injustice is really the patience of His redeeming grace. We do not understand why God does not "zap" the Hitlers, the Stalins, the Bin Ladens, and the other murderers of this world, but God loves the perpetrator of a crime just as He loves the victim. God loves everyone, not just the "good folks" (John 3:16). The Lord's heart breaks every time a person dies without having a personal relationship with Him through Christ (2 Pet. 3:9). Every lost person is dear to God even though he rejects Him. The lost one will spend eternity separated from God, but He never stops loving him.

Job learned that we do not need to understand everything. The issue is not why things happen, but whether we can trust God. Job's resounding answer is yes, we can trust Him. God's love is constant. He is always faithful.

Endnotes

1 From "How Great Thou Art" by Stuart K. Hine (Valencia, CA: Manna Music, 1953).

Chapter 13

When Wisdom Comes

Job 32:6–9

Young Elihu stood in the background during the debates between Job and his three friends. Elihu had come to give comfort and counsel to Job, but out of respect for their age he listened quietly as his elders carried on their dialogues. When he finally spoke, he was intense and prophetic. Elihu's declaration rang with profound meaning: "I am young in years, while you are old; therefore I was timid and afraid to tell you what I know. I thought that age should speak and maturity should teach wisdom. But it is a spirit in man and the breath of the Almighty that give him understanding. It is not only the old who are wise, or the elderly who understand how to judge" (Job 32:6–9).

Wisdom is not automatically acquired. We acquire wisdom when we learn the lessons that God gives to us each day. Each day is an opportunity to learn about God, ourselves, and the world in which we live. Thus Psalm 90:12 says, "Teach us to number our days carefully so that we may develop wisdom in our hearts." We need to be taught.

Each new day says something to us. Our days have a voice, for Psalm 19:1–2 says: "The heavens declare the glory of God, and the sky proclaims the work of His hands. Day after day they pour out speech; night after night they communicate knowledge." Jesus said, "Anyone who has ears to hear should listen" (Luke 14:35). We must be willing to listen. We must not waste a single day, for each one brings a reminder of God's love and grace.

Some days are full of joy and "mountaintop" experiences. We are happy and buoyant. Everything seems to be going our way, and the future looks bright. Those days tell us to bless the name of the Lord. We should praise and thank the Lord for His grace and mercy.

Some days are filled with sorrow. These days of sadness may teach us that God cares for us. First Peter 5:7 speaks of "casting all of your care upon Him, because He cares about you" and 2 Corinthians 1:3–4 refers to God as "the Father of mercies and God of all comfort, He comforts us in all our affliction."

God gives grace, mercy, and strength for days of achievement and days of failure, days of health and days of illness. Days of health teach us to work because "night is coming when no one can work" (John 9:4). Days of illness teach us to seek the Lord in adversity.

God speaks to us all through life. When we are young and exuberant, God reveals truths to us that He wants us to respond to with youthful vigor and enthusiasm. We may listen, but often only from the perspective of youth—we tend to think that we will live forever.

When we are more mature, we experience the sobering effects of caring for our families, establishing our vocations, and putting down our roots. Our middle years remind us of the importance of living consistently for the Lord.

In time the golden years come and remind us of the reality of eternity. We realize then the need to live every day fully and grasp the opportunities that God gives us. No matter how old we grow, each new day is a reminder that God wants to speak to our hearts in a special way to achieve His purposes in our lives.

The cumulative effect of all our days is the "multitude of years" that comprise our age. Even in old age we can learn something new and fresh about God and His ways every day. But sometimes the passing of days robs us of our closeness to God. Elihu put his finger on this basic problem that people may encounter as they grow older.

When Job reacted arrogantly to the false charges of his friends, Elihu caught the shift in Job's attitude. Job had started out with his heart right before God, but the more he suffered, the more anger and bitterness he displayed. Elihu condemned Job because he was proud of his righteousness (which did not really exist). Elihu also rejected the counsel of Job's three older friends because they condemned Job without offering any evidence.

As the years come and go, they sometimes rob us of our strength, innocence, and purity. If this happens, we may grow cold toward God. If we were honest, many of us would have to admit, "There was a day when I loved God more than I love Him now. There was a time when God was more precious to me than He is today. There was a day when I was more excited about my faith than I am today. There was a day when I was more filled with His power and presence."

Normally we do not take giant steps away from God. We do not go quickly from being filled with the Spirit and walking in His presence to being involved in gross immorality. We lost our closeness to God one day at a time—by going a day without prayer, by going a day without reflecting on God's goodness, by going a day without studying His word. Another day comes and we are just as neglectful. Pretty soon two days become a week, a week becomes a month, and months become years. Step by step we draw away from God. Usually the process is so gradual we do not even realize that we have lost our closeness to God. Before long we may be basking in worldliness.

When Moses came down from Mount Sinai where he had talked with God, his face was so radiant that he had to cover it with a veil. He continued to wear the veil so that the Israelites could look at him steadily, but neither he nor they were sensitive to the fact that the glory was gradually fading away (Exod. 34:29–35; 2 Cor. 3:7–18). When we take small steps away from God, the glory of His presence in our lives fades away indiscernibly. That is why it is important for us to listen to God every day. When we daily observe His lessons, we will acquire wisdom as we age.

We need to be sensitive to God's instruction as we move through life. Growing old is automatic, but growing wise is not. It requires the discipline of applying the lessons of every day so we may stay close to God. Knowing the importance of these daily lessons and their rewards, the psalmist wrote: "How can a young man keep his way pure? By keeping Your word. I have sought You with all my heart; don't let me wander from Your commands. I have treasured Your word in my heart so that I man not sin against You. Lord, may You be praised; teach me Your statues" (Ps. 119:9–12). The lessons of our days help us to grow in wisdom and draw us nearer to God.

Let us think for a moment of all the things we learn in life. The accumulation of experiences should make us grow in wisdom. Like a snowball getting bigger as it rolls down a slope, we should become wiser as we move through life. We should know more this year than we did last year. As we learn the lessons God teaches us day by day, we should grow spiritually.

As we grow, we learn that we cannot trust ourselves. How many times have we done things we vowed we would never do? There is no sin we could not commit. Around us we see a world that is perverse and corrupt, and if we look inside ourselves, we see the same things in our hearts. That is why Jeremiah 17:9 says, "The heart is more deceitful than anything else and desperately sick."

We also learn that we *can* trust God. When we experience a dark day, we may conclude that life is collapsing around us. But then we reach the other side of the valley and see that God was in our experience. A dark day can become one of the best things that ever happened to us if we learn to trust God in it. We learn that He is faithful and will keep His word.

As we grow in wisdom, we gain spiritual insight. The word of God illuminates our hearts and minds. We become more sensitive to the presence of the Spirit of God in our lives. Spiritual insight makes us more realistic about ourselves and thus makes us see our need to avoid the people and places associated with our besetting sins. We become more intent on serving and pleasing God and doing His will.

We become wiser about Satan as we grow spiritually. Satan has not changed his tactics; he is still alive and aggressive. The devil and his disciples have a great deal of courage, zeal, and enthusiasm, and they are always busy. So we take the advice of 1 Peter 5:8: "Be sober! Be on the alert! Your adversary the Devil is prowling around like a roaring, lion, looking for anyone he can devour." Becoming smarter about our warfare with Satan, we follow the instruction of Ephesians 6:11–12: "Put on the full armor of God so that you can stand against the tactics of the Devil For our battle is not against flesh and blood, but against the rulers, against the authorities, against the world powers of this darkness, against the spiritual forces of evil in the heavens."

As we grow in wisdom, we become more yielded to the Holy Spirit, who teaches us. Remember Elihu said, "It is a spirit in man and the breath of the Almighty that give him understanding" (Job 32:8). Jesus told the disciples, "When the Spirit of truth comes, He will guide you into all truth" (John 16:13). When we commit each day to God and submit to His leadership, we are anointed by the Holy Spirit, who illuminates our hearts and minds and teaches us God's lessons. As we yield to Him, God the Holy Spirit guides us and gives us understanding of God's word.

If we apply the lessons of our days and acquire wisdom as we grow older, we should pass on our knowledge. Elihu said, "I thought that age should speak and maturity should teach wisdom" (Job 32:7). God expects those of us to whom God gives length of life and a storehouse of wisdom to teach others. We receive; thus we give. That is God's pattern (2 Tim. 2:2). God instructs us so that we can instruct others. So many Christians today want to be taught, but they do not understand that they cannot really be taught unless they teach. We do not learn our daily lessons unless we give what we learn to others.

Paul's letter to Titus reminds us who have been taught that we ought to teach others. Titus was helping to organize newly established churches in Crete, and Paul instructed him to use the older women to teach the younger women (Titus 2:3–5). The apostle knew that truth cannot be radiated; it must be communicated.

Someone said, "The only debt we owe to the past is to leave the future indebted to us." It is our responsibility to share what our experiences have taught us, just as we have learned from the experiences of others. We have learned from the examples of people in the Bible and history books, and we are still learning from God's faithful servants who today are passing on to others the great lessons He is teaching them through their daily experiences.

We can learn a lesson from a Filipino evangelist about whom John Corts wrote. Corts, director of Billy Graham's "Amsterdam '83" and "Amsterdam '86" conferences on evangelism, reported that the Filipino requested one hundred thousand New Testaments. His letter stated, "I must have them, and I must have them within the next six months." When asked why he needed one hundred thousand he answered, "Because I can distribute one hundred thousand in the Philippines in the next six months." When asked how he would carry one hundred thousand New Testaments, he replied, "I just carry them on my back."

Over the next couple of months the Filipino's references were checked and letters were exchanged about his ministry. Finally Corts received a letter saying, "You've written a number of letters, and already a couple of months have gone by. Don't you understand it is urgent that this man get those one hundred thousand New Testaments?" When Corts inquired about the reason for the urgency, the correspondent explained that the man, who was eighty-one years old, had terminal cancer and the doctors had told him he had only six months to live. His time was running out.

That Filipino evangelist had learned about God's love, and he wanted to share it with a lost and dying world. What a lesson we can learn from him! We can learn from his example about the urgency of spreading the gospel to those for whom Christ died. We can learn about expending some of the love we have been given, about reflecting some of the love we have been given, about reflecting the heart of God who "loved the world in this way: He gave His One and Only Son, so that everyone who believes in Him will not perish but have eternal life" (John 3:16).

We will all grow older until we die. But we will only grow wiser if we make the Holy Spirit welcome in our hearts and allow the breath of the Almighty to teach us the lessons of our days. Each day is a unique day—it will never come again—so we must learn its lesson.

We have a tendency to think that we will always have many more opportunities and much more time. But we only have today. God has given us this marvelous moment in which to live for Him. We must make the most of it and follow the instruction of Ephesians 5:15–16 that directs us, "Pay careful attention, then, to how you walk not as unwise people but as wise making the most of the time because the days are evil." If we would do something for God, we must do it now. If we have learned something that we should share, we must share it now. That is the message we hear when wisdom comes.

Chapter 14

Seeing God's Hand in Everything

Job 12:9–10

Job's friends came to comfort him but ended up criticizing him and accusing him. Reasoning incorrectly, they hastily concluded that Job was afflicted because of his sin. Although some individuals do suffer as a result of their sin, this was not true in Job's case. His suffering was not due to a broken relationship with God.

As Job defended himself, he demonstrated a most exciting truth that is universally proclaimed throughout all creation: The presence of God is involved in every experience, in every circumstance.

> Ask the animals, and they will instruct you;
> Ask the birds of the sky, and they will tell you
> Or speak to the earth, and it will instruct you;
> Let the fish of the sea inform you
> Which of all these does not know
> That the hand of the Lord has done this?
> The life of every living thing is in His hand,
> As well as the breath of all mankind? (Job 12:7–10).

If we put this truth into our hearts, plant it in our minds, and let it abide within us, it will revolutionize our lives. This truth can change our attitudes and give us victory in the midst of every circumstance.

Everything that comes to us in life comes through the hand of God. God does not cause everything, but He permits everything that comes to us. Knowing that God is ultimately involved in everything in our lives should change our whole outlook on life and give us victory in distress. Although we cannot always recognize His presence, God is with us, and He is guiding us.

Job spoke of animals, birds, fish, and the earth itself declaring the presence of God. We cannot go anywhere in God's creation without finding evidence of His presence (Ps. 19:1; 97:6). The word of God clearly states that God is omnipresent.

Psalm 139:7–10 says, "Where can I go to escape Your Spirit? Where can I flee from Your presence? If I go up to heaven, You are there; if I make my bed in Sheol, You are there. If I live at the eastern horizon or settle at the western limits, even there Your hand will lead me; Your right hand will hold on to me." Wherever we go, God is there. The fact is obvious, yet some people deliberately obscure that truth in their hearts as they try to blot God out of their minds.

The presence of God and the power of God are inseparable. God is busy working everywhere. He is always awake and never idle. Psalm 121:1–4 teaches this truth: "I raise my eyes toward the mountains. Where will my help come from? My help comes from the Lord, the Maker of heaven and earth. He will not allow your foot to slip; your Protector will not slumber. Indeed, the Protector of Israel does not slumber or sleep."

In every place, in every time, and in every event of our lives, God is fully present in power. The power of God—the hand of God—is in everything. Job asked, "Which of all these does not know that the hand of the Lord has done this?" (Job 12:9). No matter where we are or what we are doing, whether we are aware of it or not, God is always with us in all of His power. This truth inspires awe and wonder in our hearts and minds. It tells us that He will never leave us or forsake us. The apostle Paul put it this way:

> Who can separate us from the love of Christ? Can affliction or anguish or persecution or famine or nakedness of danger or sword? ... No, in all these things we are more than victorious through Him who loved us. For I am persuaded that neither death nor life, nor angels nor rulers, nor things present, nor things to come, nor powers, nor height, nor depth, nor any other created thing will have the power to separate us from the love of God that is in Christ Jesus our Lord! (Rom. 8:35, 37–39).

The presence and the power of God are with us in *happy times* when the sun is shining. He is there when we are successful and everything seems to be going our way. Sometimes we are not grateful for God's presence during the good times because we think the good times are a result of something we have done. We tend to think that prosperity is a result of our spirituality—until we lose our prosperity.

We often take our prosperity or our health for granted until we lose it. Then we are grateful for the prosperity or the health we had before it was lost. Sometimes we are not grateful for our families until we lose them. Divorce or death or some other tragedy intrudes, and then we learn to appreciate the family unit. During good times we may take our loved ones and our blessings for granted. We may not give them a thought until something goes wrong.

Often we do not give God a thought either, or at least not a second thought, while things are going well. However, it is important for us to acknowledge the presence and the power of God in good times. It is important to attribute the happy times to God. Remember, "Every generous act and every perfect gift is from above, coming down from the Father of lights; with Him there is no variation or shadow cast by turning" (James 1:17). God provides the good things we enjoy.

The preacher in Ecclesiastes also recognized the presence and power of God in happy times. He wrote: "There is nothing better for man than to eat, drink, and to enjoy his work. I have seen that even this is from God's hand" (Eccles. 2:24).

God's presence and power are also with us in *trying times* when we face difficulties and disappointments. The book of Genesis illustrates this truth in the story of Joseph. He was the second-youngest son of Jacob. His older brothers, who hated him so much that they wanted to kill him, sold him to a group of Midianite traders en route to Egypt. The brothers then killed a goat, dipped Joseph's tunic in the blood, and convinced Jacob that Joseph had been killed by a wild animal.

In Egypt Joseph worked as a slave for Potiphar, who was an officer in the Egyptian army. Joseph pleased his employer and became the master of Potiphar's household. But when Joseph rejected the advances of Potiphar's wife, she falsely accused him of impropriety, and he was cast into prison. During three years of confinement, Joseph rose to a position of leadership among the prisoners. He was delivered from prison when God enabled him to interpret the dreams of the pharaoh, and ultimately Joseph became the second most powerful man in all of Egypt.

Under Joseph's leadership the Egyptians were able to gather enough food to prepare for the famine that Joseph predicted. Because of the stockpile of grain of the silos of Egypt, Joseph's brothers traveled from Israel to purchase grain after the famine wiped out their reserves. Joseph's brothers were brought before him, and the resulting scene is one of the most emotional moments in human history. Joseph saw his brothers and hid his face because he was overwhelmed. We would have expected him to savor the moment when he could reveal himself to his brothers and take advantage of his position. Revenge could have been his. He could have repaid his brothers for their malicious actions toward him many years earlier. Instead he spoke of how God had used his brothers to accomplish His purpose:

> And now don't be worried or angry with yourselves for selling me here, because God sent me ahead of you to preserve life ... God sent me ahead of you to establish you as a remnant within the land and to keep you alive by a great deliverance. Therefore it was not you who sent me here, but God. He has made me a father to Pharaoh, lord of his entire household, and ruler over all the land of Egypt (Gen. 45:5, 7–8).

In Joseph's most difficult experiences, God's sovereign hand was working out His marvelous plan. Joseph was aware of the presence and the power of God during the trying times as well as the happy times.

When Jacob died, Joseph's brothers were afraid that he would retaliate against them for what they had done to him. Again Joseph's forgiving heart revealed itself when he said, "Don't be afraid. Am I in the place of God? You planned evil against me; God planned it for good to bring about the present result the survival of many people" (Gen. 50:19–20).

The story of Joseph reminds us of the glorious truth that God is present in His power—whether we are aware of it or not—when we face times of disappointment, despair, pressure, and deterioration.

God's presence and power are with us even in *rebellious times*. God does not leave us even when we rebel against Him as the prodigal son rebelled against his father. Many of us feel that we can avoid God by running away from Him, but He stays with us.

Genesis 13–19 includes an account of God's presence and power at work in the life of a rebellious young man named Lot. Lot had become wealthy while living and working with his uncle Abraham, but when Lot's employees began to strive with Abraham's men, it became necessary for them to separate. Abraham gave Lot first choice of grazing lands, and Lot chose the one that showed the most promise, the plain of Jordan. He moved toward the cities of the plain and as time passed became involved with the people of Sodom. Eventually Lot became one of the leaders of the city. He had attached himself to the wicked people of Sodom and Gomorrah.

In the meantime God had been watching the growing wickedness of Sodom and Gomorrah, and He decided to destroy them. But because of Abraham's intercession, God sent angelic messengers to rescue rebellious Lot. Lot's wife died as the family fled the destruction of Sodom. Lot and his two daughters were the only survivors of the holocaust.

From the biblical record we learn that Lot was a young believer who rebelled against God. He did wrong things and associated with the wrong people. Yet even during Lot's rebellious years, God's presence and power were present in his life. Likewise when we rebel against God, He is present in our lives and His power preserves us. Even when we push away from what God wants us to do and we are not interested in Him, God's power is at work in our lives. What a comfort that truth is for us, especially if we have loved ones who are in rebellion against God.

God's presence and power are with us in happy times, trying times, rebellious times—and in seemingly *insignificant times*. We expect God to be involved in the cataclysmic experiences of life, in its great triumphs and tragedies. But perhaps the most exciting time to experience God's presence and power is the insignificant moment. God is involved in every breath we draw (Job 12:9–10).

We can discover God in our mundane, everyday, ordinary experiences. Our lives are made up of countless trifles. Big moments are few and far between. The ordinary details of life drive us to distraction and depression and often cause more trouble than the big catastrophes.

God is interested in the insignificant times of our lives. He is so interested in our day-to-day existence that he has assigned angels to watch over us. Psalm 91:11–12 declares: "For He will give His angels orders concerning you, to protect you in all your ways. They will support you with their hands so that you will not strike your foot against a stone." God says that angels will keep us from stubbing our toes. What a wonder! God has given angels the task of keeping us from problems caused by insignificant things. Many times the angels guide and protect us without our awareness.

Jesus said: "Aren't two sparrows sold for a penny? Yet not one of them falls to the ground without your Father's consent. But even the hairs of your head have all been counted. Don't be afraid therefore; you are worth more than many sparrows" (Matt. 10:29–31). Notice Jesus did not say eagle. He said sparrow. The sparrow is small and insignificant, almost worthless in comparison to other birds. That is why Jesus used the sparrow in His illustration. If God is concerned about sparrows, how much more must He care about us!

Some things that seem insignificant to other people are important to us. A teenager once approached me with a question that loomed large in his mind. He wanted to know if God was interested in whether he had a girlfriend. Adults may think his question was silly, but God did not laugh. I assured him that God was interested in his desire to have a girlfriend. God is interested in all the things that seem important to us as well as all the things that we think are insignificant. If God only answered us when we were in trouble, we would be pitiful indeed. Our God is the provider and sustainer for every experience of life.

God cares about all mankind, not just some of us. Notice the inclusive language in Job 12:10. God, who is omnipresent and omnipotent, stands by all of us in every moment of our lives. We can count on it.

God holds the soul of every living person in His hands for a purpose. What is that purpose? A popular answer today is that God created us for the purpose of fellowship. We do have fellowship with God and we praise Him for it, but that was not God's purpose in creation. Man was created to give glory to God.

God was not incomplete in Himself, nor was He a sociologically lonely being. In His eternal existence the triune God was fully satisfied and fulfilled in fellowship within the godhead. God did not need us. The eternal godhead was complete and fulfilled before the creation. John 1:1–4 describes the pre-existing relationship between God the Father and God the Word (Jesus Christ): "In the beginning was the Word, and the Word was with God, and the Word was God. He was with God in the beginning. All things were created through Him, and apart from Him not one thing was created that has been created. Life was in Him, and that life was the light of men." God through Jesus Christ created us so that we would be a reflection of His glory.

Elsewhere we read about Jesus Christ, that He is "the radiance of His glory, the exact expression of His nature" (Heb. 1:3). The radiance is inseparable from deity itself because Jesus Christ is God. The apostle Paul wrote, "He is the image of the invisible God," and went on to say, "For in Him the entire fullness of God's nature dwells bodily, and you have been filled by Him, who is the head over every ruler and authority" (Col. 1:15; 2:9–10).

We are to be like Jesus, who radiates God's glory. God created us in order to glorify Himself. As we fulfill that purpose, we have the privilege of being in fellowship with God. Fellowship with God, in other words, is the result, not the purpose, of our creation.

Every person is to bring glory to God—not just preachers, missionaries, or evangelists. And not just Christians have this purpose. Proverbs 21:1 says, "A king's heart is a water channel in the Lord's hand: He directs it wherever He chooses." God directs the waters from the highlands to the sea, and He achieves His purpose even through pagan kings who do not love God or acknowledge Him. God, who has the power to turn a king's heart at His will, has a purpose in this world that no government can thwart. Just as He used pagan kings to accomplish His will in Bible times, He can turn the hearts of godless leaders in America and around the world today in order to accomplish His purpose in the lives of all mankind.

This universal truth is precious to those of us who are saved. God not only has a purpose for the world in general. He also has a purpose for us in particular. That fact ought to motivate us to trust Him and to obey Him in everything.

When we as God's children recognize the presence, power, and purpose of God in all things, we can have confidence in Him. Job went through deep waters, but he learned to trust God. Recognizing the hand of God in his life, he affirmed a tremendous confidence in Him: "Even if He kills me, I will hope in Him" (Job 13:15). Nothing could stop him from trusting God.

Job did not say, "Though I die, yet will I trust Him." Death is not a pleasant thought for any of us, but Job was not just speaking about death; he was talking about God. Job declared that if God were to take a dagger and plunge it into his heart, he would still trust Him. When his faith was tested, Job put that rest into an eternal perspective. His faith went beyond the grave.

Our faith will be tested too. It has to be tested, for how can we know what kind of faith we have if it is not tested? It was tested in the life of our Savior, so we can be sure it will be tested in our lives. "For it was fitting, in bringing many sons to glory, that He, for whom and through whom all things exist, should make the source of their salvation perfect through sufferings" (Heb. 2:10).

The real question of the book of Job is, "Does anyone serve God just because He is God and not because of what He does?" Job certainly answered that question when he declared, "Even if He kills me, I will hope in Him." His response illustrates the difference between the children of the world and the children of God. The children of the world come to the point of testing with despair, whereas the children of God come to this point with trust in God.

When there is nowhere else to turn, those of us who are God's children turn in faith to our heavenly Father. When we are not conscious of any comfort or response to our prayers, we still trust God. Many people today do not have such strong faith. They have faith as long as things are going their way. But when something happens that they did not want to happen, they blame God. Things were not going Job's way, but in those trials he affirmed that nothing would cause him to lose his trust in God.

Why was Job able to speak with such bold confidence? The answer is simple. Job knew God and had committed his life to Him. Job believed God because he knew Him personally and experientially. Even if God did something unthinkable to him, Job would still trust Him.

How can we develop a confidence like Job's? We must remember that it is difficult for a stranger to trust God. To trust Him implicitly, we must know God personally. Psalm 9:10 says, "Those who know Your name trust in You." When we know God personally and commit our lives to Him, we will trust Him regardless of what He allows to come into our lives.

Chapter 15

Longing for the Good Old Days

Job 29:2–6

Job had time on his hands during his affliction. His friends who came to comfort him waited a whole week before speaking to him. He apparently spent a great deal of time thinking about his life. As he reflected on his past, Job longed for the good old days:

> If only I could be as in months gone by, in the days when God watched over me, when His lamp shone above my head, and I walked through darkness by His light! I would be as I was in the days of my youth when God's friendship rested on my tent, when the Almighty was still with me and my children were around me, when my feet were bathed in cream and the rock poured out streams of oil for me (Job 29:2–6)!

In his distress surely Job thought about the times of his prosperity, but he also pondered over his relationship with God. His spiritual life was strained, and he thought about the state of his heart as well as the loss of his possessions. His soul was depressed, for he had lost the light of God's countenance upon his face.

Losses Sustained

Many of us can remember a time when our faith was stronger and God seemed more real to us than He does today. We remember when God's presence was more precious to us. Job remembered when he had walked in the light of God's presence and he had God's wisdom for the decisions he needed to make. He no longer possessed the exuberance of faith and the enthusiasm about God and life that he once had. He had lost his awareness of God's providence, provision, protection, and purpose.

Job Lost His Awareness of God's Providence

Job said, "If only it could be as … in the days when God watched over me" (Job 29:2). There had been a time when Job was confident of God's guiding hand upon his life. He had been able to see how God protected him from sin, and he had been aware that God's providential care was like a hedge around him. Conscious of the work of God's Spirit, Job had readily obeyed and followed Him without question. Now, however, Job had lost his awareness of God's providence.

The word of God teaches that God's providential care is at work in the lives of believers. Jeremiah wrote: "'For I know the plans I have for you' this is the Lord's declaration 'plans for your welfare, not for disaster, to give you a future and a hope'" (Jer. 29:11).

The essence of eternal life is that we can never be separated from God and His love. What blessed assurance we have when we place our lives in the hands of Christ Jesus!

> Loved with everlasting love,
> Led by grace that love to know;

Gracious Spirit from above,
Thou hast taught me it is so!
O, this full and perfect peace!
O, the transport all divine!
In a love which cannot cease,
I am His, and He is mine![1]

Job Lost His Awareness of God's Provision

Job described a time "when His lamp shone upon my head" (Job 29:3). The sun of God's provision had shone brightly on Job, and he had rejoiced in it. Before his afflictions he would rise early "in the morning and offer burnt offerings for all of them ... this was Job's regular practice" (Job 1:5). That was an exciting time in his life and spiritual pilgrimage.

When he received repeated reports about the tragic destruction of his family and possessions, "Then Job stood up, tore his robe and shaved his head. He fell to the ground and worshiped ... Throughout all this Job did not sin or blame God for anything" (Job 1:20–22). Even in the face of these losses, the peace of God was a constant factor in his life. The sun of God's love was so brilliant that it shone upon him without casting a single shadow. Victory and triumph were reflected in his life. When he lost his health and his wife responded bitterly, Job said, "Should we accept only good from God and not adversity?" (Job 2:10). But after his friends came and bombarded him with accusations and criticisms, Job wore down under the stress. He lost his awareness of God's provision.

We do not need to wear down under stress, for Jesus said, "Don't worry about your life, what you will eat or what you will drink; or about your body, what you will wear. Isn't life more than food and the body more than clothing? ... But seek first the Kingdom of God and His righteousness, and all these things will be provided for you" (Matt. 6:25, 33). Paul wrote from prison, "My God will supply all your needs according to His riches in glory in Christ Jesus" (Phil. 4:19). When we are in His hands, we can rest in the awareness of His provision.

Job Lost His Awareness of God's Protection

Job expressed his sense of vulnerability when he said, "I walked through darkness by His light" (Job 29:3). This statement described a time in Job's life when God's light had shone so brightly on him that he knew where to go. The presence of God had been so illuminating that he knew which steps to take and when to take them. He had walked in close communion with God.

Now he could no longer sense God's presence and protection. The darkness of alienation from family and friends filled him with despair. Unable to see God's light on his path, he stumbled in the darkness.

When we walk through darkness, we have a sense of imminent danger, for we are more prone to injury than we are when we can see what is in front of us. In the darkness we are likely to take steps we should not take. We are apt to make harmful mistakes, so we need God's protection.

In the darkness we are prone to fear, so we need to be aware of God's protection. We can find security in scripture written to believers who were about to go through persecution because of their faith in Jesus Christ: "[The Lord] Himself has said, 'I will never leave you nor forsake you.' Therefore, we may boldly say: 'The Lord is my helper; I will not be afraid. What can man do to me?'" (Heb. 13:5–6). When we place our trust in the person of Jesus Christ, He will protect us.

When we go through difficult times and feel overwhelmed by circumstances beyond our control, we can rest in the assuring words God gave to Paul: "My grace is sufficient for you, for power is perfected in weakness" (2 Cor. 12:9). No pain or circumstance of this life can ever defeat those who are in Christ.

Job Lost His Awareness of God's Purpose

Job 29:4 expresses loss of the awareness of God's purpose: "I would be as I was in the days of my youth when God's friendship rested on my tent." When Job was young and idealistic, he was aware of God's presence and God's will. In his youth Job had a sense of mission and saw the things of God clearly. He had enthusiasm, exuberance, and a "can do" spirit.

Although we cannot be certain what "God's friendship" was, it probably referred to Job's purity of heart and purpose, when God's presence was strong in his life. When Job was young, God showed Job the secrets of His heart. Job saw the purpose of God for his life and committed himself to it. No wonder Job longed for the good old days.

Many in the church today identify with Job, for they can think back to a time when God's purpose was the most important thing in the world to them. Like Job, they feel they have lost the song that once rang in their hearts, the excitement that once bubbled over in their lives. They have lost the sense of God's presence and the unbridled delight of doing His will. Many have gone astray, and all they can do is long for the good old days.

The story of Simon Peter and the other disciples illustrates this feeling of loss in the life of a child of God. We can trace the steps Peter took as he lost his keen sensitivity to the things of God. First, when Jesus needed the disciples to watch while He prayed in the garden, they fell asleep. When Jesus was betrayed and needed them to stand with Him and encourage Him, "they all deserted Him and ran away" (Mark 14:50). At first Peter had tried to defend Christ (Mark 14:47), but now he "followed Him at a distance" (Mark 14:54). There was a time when he was not ashamed of Jesus, but now Peter backed away from the Lord; he was no longer in the battle.

Peter's steps away from God continued in the high priest's courtyard where he denied Christ three times. "I do not know this Man you are talking about!" he said (Mark 14:71). The rooster crowed and Peter remembered that Jesus had said he would deny Him three times before the rooster crowed. At that very moment Jesus emerged from His trial and looked at Peter (Luke 22:61). That look must have spoken volumes to the heart of Peter, for he "went outside and wept bitterly" (Luke 22:62).

Try to imagine the pain and hurt of the Savior who had devoted His life to His disciples. He had called them, loved them, trained them, and equipped them. Now when He was suffering and dying for them, they fled. Even Simon Peter, who had declared, "You are the Messiah, the Son of the living God" (Matt. 16:16), had turned his back on Him. All that hurt must have been reflected in His look at Peter.

Peter had lost his closeness to his Lord. Now, like Job, Peter could only remember when times were different. He could only recall the intimacy he had shared before the breach in his fellowship with the Lord.

Why did the disciples forsake Christ? Why did Peter deny Jesus so strongly? Certainly they were afraid. Jesus was under arrest and was being tried by the authorities. But fear never comes from God. Second Timothy 1:7 says, "For God has not given us a spirit of fearfulness, but one of power, love, and sound judgment." And 1 John 4:18–19 says, "There is no fear in love; instead, perfect love casts out fear, because fear involves punishment. So the one who fears has not reached perfection in love. We love because He first loved us." Whenever we have fear, we know it is not from God. Fear always comes from Satan. Nevertheless, fear was one reason the disciples forsook Jesus.

Weakness was another reason the disciples fled. They were weak in the flesh, yet they were self-confident and cocky. They thought they would never forsake Jesus! Hadn't they all pledged their lives to Him? They were sure of themselves and had not yet learned that without Jesus they could do nothing. The important lesson for us here is that we need to learn to distrust ourselves. We need the strength that comes from time spent alone with God and His word and the encouragement of Christian fellowship (Heb. 10:25).

Unless we are constantly vigilant and deliberately maintain our focus on God, we drift aimlessly away from Him. Unless we consciously obey God, we begin to push His will aside. Our love for God cools, and our enthusiasm for His work fades. We set out on a journey without God's guidance and discover too late that we are somewhere we do not want to be. The destination is not worth the trip.

God has a worthwhile destination for us. To reach it we must be diligent about guarding our spiritual lives and our love for the Lord. The problem of maintaining diligence is addressed in Revelation 2:2–5, where John recorded what the Spirit said to the church at Ephesus:

> I know your works, your labor, and your endurance, and that you cannot tolerate evil. You have tested those who call themselves apostles and are not, and you have found them to be liars. You also possess endurance and have tolerated many things because of My name, and have not grown weary. But I have this against you: you have abandoned the love you had at first. Remember then how far you have fallen; repent, and do the works you did at first. Otherwise, I will come to you and remove your lampstand from its place unless you repent.

Awareness Regained

Perhaps some of us have not maintained our diligence, and we have lost our first love. We have lost our awareness of the presence of God. If we have sustained this loss, how can we do more than just long for the good old days? How can we regain our closeness with the Lord? How did the disciples come back into fellowship with Jesus?

1. The disciples surrendered to His will. We can pattern our renewal after the disciples' by recognizing any areas of our lives that are out of

God's will and surrendering them. The disciples had been unwilling to let Jesus "go away." (Remember His gentle explanation in John 16:4–7.) But as they surrendered to God's plan, even though they did not fully understand it, God brought great fellowship, power, and effectiveness to their lives.

Until we surrender to His will, we will only be able to remember the good old days. We will be out of fellowship as long as our actions dishonor Him. Until we confess our disobedience, we will not regain our former closeness to God. Once we admit that things are not what they once were, we can do something about it (1 John 1:9).

We need to surrender our wills to God and be led by His Spirit. If we do not quench the Spirit (1 Thess. 5:19) or grieve the Spirit (Eph. 4:30), we will regain our awareness of the presence of God.

2. *The disciples were determined in prayer.* The disciples prayed for ten days after they became aware of their weak spiritual condition. They prayed together in the upper room from the time they returned from the ascension until the day of Pentecost. With one accord they awaited the fulfillment of the Lord's promise of the dynamic power that would enable them to witness throughout the world.

When we lose fellowship with God, we need to spend time with God in prayer. If we are to be restored to our previous position with God and regain an awareness of His work in our lives, we must become serious about prayer; through prayer the disciples were able to renew their personal communication with the Lord. Job also regained his awareness of the Lord through personal, determined prayer. It is the basic step.

3. *The disciples appropriated his power.* Jesus had told the disciples, "And look, I am sending you what My Father promised. As for you stay in the city until you are empowered from on high" (Luke 24:49). There, after they surrendered their hearts to His will and determined to pray for the Promise, the Holy Spirit came upon them as "a violent rushing wind" (Acts 2:2) and indwelt them in a new and special way. Following

this infilling, the disciples witnessed with great power concerning the gospel of Christ. As they appropriated the power of the Holy Spirit, great grace and power flowed through their lives, and they were able to perform miracle after miracle.

When we appropriate His power, we can have our first love for the Lord restored. We can recapture that spirit of closeness and warmth. We can come to the place of fellowship again. (See Acts 4:31–33.)

We need to do more than long for the good old days. We need to surrender to His will, determine to be individuals of prayer, and appropriate His power in our lives. God does not want us to exist longing for the bygone days. He wants us to rededicate ourselves with the vigor of our first love. Then we will regain what was ours in the past.

By the end of the book of Job, Job had come into a new and vital experience with God. He did more than go back to where he was before his life fell apart. He gained an awareness of God that was deeper and richer than anything he had experienced in the good old days. Job said to the Lord: "I had heard rumors about You, but no my eyes have seen You. Therefore I take back my words and repent in dust and ashes" (Job 42:5–6). Job had a new depth to his relationship with God. The future was better than the past.

There could not have been a new dimension to Job's life with God, however, without a new commitment. And for us there can be no fresh start unless we repent. We will never do more than long for the good old days unless we once again turn away from ourselves and our sin to the Savior. When we recommit our lives to Him, we can recapture the time when God was real and Jesus was precious. And we can rebuild our relationship with God with new exuberance and excitement, for the old days are only shadows of greater things to come. Surely the best is yet to be!

Endnotes

1 From the hymn, "I Am His, and He Is Mine," by George W. Robinson.

Chapter 16
When a Man Sees God

Job 42:5-6

Everyone has faith in something. Everyone begins with a basic premise. The atheist may say, "There is no God," but he believes in himself, and on that basic premise he builds his humanistic philosophy. Everyone builds his world view, religion, or philosophy on a basic premise. The basic premise of the Christian is faith in God.

Job's Basic Premises

Job had two basic premises on which he constructed his worldview. His first premise was faith in God's power and sovereignty. He said, "I know that You can do anything and no plan of Yours can be thwarted" (Job 42:2).

We all have a choice to believe (like Job) or not to believe (like the atheist) in the existence, power, and sovereignty of God. As finite creatures we can never fully approach God with our intellects, but if we start with the premise of faith, we will be able to find understanding. We could never completely understand all there is to know about the infinite Creator, but we do not have to know everything about God in order to believe in Him. The fact that we are limited in our ability to understand does not mean that the Christian faith is illogical or irrational. It is reasonable to accept God and His authority as part of our philosophical database.

Job's second premise was his own inadequacy. He said, "Surely I spoke about things I did not understand, things too wonderful for me to know" (Job 42:3). When the Lord spoke out of the whirlwind He asked, "Who is this who obscures My counsel with ignorant words?" (Job 38:2). In 42:3 Job was responding to that question. In essence he said, "I am that foolish man who uttered what he did not understand."

Job had sounded off when he knew nothing about the big picture. When he was challenged to compare his own capabilities with the capabilities of God, he was astounded. Job confessed his own inadequacy in the face of the mysteries of life and the mastery of God over them. This heart attitude made it possible for Job to grow in stature before God. As a result of his spiritual growth he was able to say to the Lord, "I had heard rumors about You, but now my eyes have seen You. Therefore I take back my words and repent in dust and ashes" (Job 42:5–6). His ultimate faith in God was an acknowledgement of God's greatness and a denial of his own ability.

We have to choose between placing our faith in ourselves and placing our faith in God. Job recognized his own inadequacy and placed his trust in the Lord's ability to control the issues of life. In effect he concluded: "I have struggled through the difficulty, discouragement, and depression of this life, and I have decided that there is a God. There is nothing God cannot do. There is no thought that can be withheld from Him. I was a foolish man. I uttered things that I did not understand. How presumptuous I was! I believe in God. I do not trust myself."

Today the humanist asserts: "I am sufficient within myself. If I cannot understand something, it does not exist. Only what is tangible in the universe has existence. Only what I can discover and discern is reality. Nothing exists outside the realm of materialism. There is no interaction between a so-called world of spirit and the world of matter. There is no such thing as divine revelation. We need to abandon what we used to call divine revelation because we have chosen to trust ourselves. There is nothing beyond the grasp of man."

The early evolutionists chose not to place their trust in God. *If there is no God,* they reasoned, *what could have happened?* They tried to construct a worldview that left God out of the picture. The individuals who developed the theory of Charles Darwin into a philosophical system were committed to naturalism and materialism and were opposed to the supernatural, including divine revelation. According to most of the laws of natural science, the theory of evolution that is taught broadly in our schools today is a contradiction. Yet its proponents place a tremendous amount of faith in the theory and rely on it as if it were fully tested and proven as scientific fact. Believing in their own ideas, they build their philosophy on the basic premise that there is no God.

All of us have to make a choice about our presuppositions. We have to decide whether our basic premise will be belief in God or belief in man. The choice is simple, but it has ultimate consequences.

Job's Dilemma

In the beginning of the book of Job we read that God held Job in high esteem and spoke favorably of him to Satan (Job 1:8–2:3). Job knew God in a general way—well enough to fear Him and to live circumspectly before Him. He had heard from God and about God, but he had not yet moved to a point of maturity in his relationship with God; he did not yet trust Him thoroughly. Then Job had a personal experience of discovery and he acknowledged, "I had heard rumors about you, but now my eyes have seen You" (Job 42:5).

Before this dramatic encounter with God, Job had accepted the prevalent beliefs of his day implicitly. He and his tree friends had accepted the traditional doctrines about the providence of God, the greatness and righteousness of God as creator and sustainer of the universe, and the reason for human suffering. Reflecting the prevailing thought of the day, Job's friends said to him, "If you get right with God, your suffering will stop."

Job faced an interesting dilemma. He had always believed the doctrine his friends were reciting, but now his beliefs were being challenged by what he was experiencing. Although Job's doctrines had been orthodox, he had not applied them personally. When tragedy struck, he discovered a credibility gap between what he had been taught and what he was thinking. Tragedy will either drive us away from God or drive us to God. In Job's case, trials drove him to God. When he came to the end of his own resources, he encountered God and saw just how insignificant he was. He repented and entered a new dimension of personal involvement with God. Like every believer, Job had two options, and because of the choice he made he moved from a secondhand to a firsthand experience with God.

The Option of Secondhand Faith

"I had heard rumors about You" (Job 42:5). Merely repeating what other people say about God has tragic consequences. For example, Pontius Pilate relied on secondhand knowledge of Jesus. This Roman had heard the rumors flying amid the religious and political turmoil in Jerusalem.

For years rumors had circulated about a coming king of the Jews. Some people believed that this king would be a secular ruler who would dethrone the Romans and set up a political kingdom. When the wise men from the East came looking for Jesus, King Herod became so fearful that this Jewish king had been born that he massacred all the male children in Bethlehem and its districts who were two years old and younger (Matt. 2:1–18).

Rumors flooded Jerusalem when Jesus began His public ministry and called men and women to enter His Kingdom. Finally Jesus was arrested, accused of insurrection, and put on trial before Pontius Pilate. During the hearing Pilate asked, "Are You the King of the Jews?" (John 18:33). Jesus answered Pilate with another question: "Are you asking this on your own, or have others told you about Me?" (John 18:34). Jesus wanted Pilate to face the real issue. He wanted to know about Pilate's sincerity. Did he really want to know, or was he just repeating the question others were asking?

That same issue faces us today. Are the songs we sing in church true to our experience, or are we merely repeating someone else's words? We may know what to say, when to sit, and when to stand in church. Our prayers may contain the language of religion. But do these words and actions spring from our own beliefs, or are we just copying other people? Is our faith firsthand or secondhand?

This issue is a timeless problem of faith. Before tragedy struck, Job merely repeated what he had heard. And today many people are content with—and even prefer—a hearsay-type religion. Secondhand religion is popular because it never sins against tradition. It never bursts out in enthusiasm or displays unorthodox behavior. It is always proper and never embarrasses anyone. It is exactly what we would expect it to be. Secondhand religion seems to be safe because it does not rock the boat. We do not have to change when we have a secondhand religious experience.

Secondhand faith is also popular because it does not place any obligations on us. It does not motivate us to risk rejection (after all, telling people about Jesus invades their privacy and might offend them). Secondhand faith lets us worship God in spirit without serving Him actively and makes no demands on our behavior. Without firsthand faith, we can make religion a spectator activity and stay inside the comfort zone of non-commitment and conformity. It is easier to listen to reports about church work than to become involved in the efforts. It is easier to leave religious activities to the pastor than to let our church responsibilities take precedence over our personal priorities. It is easier to deal with God by proxy than to deal with Him personally.

Secondhand faith may not make any demands, but neither does it provide any satisfaction. It is a quick recipe for misery because it has no depth of personal meaning. When we come to the end of our own strength, secondhand faith does not give us the strength of God (2 Cor. 12:9). If we can only repeat what we have heard, we will always be at the mercy of our doubts, and we will never be secure in our beliefs. If we have to rely on the experience of someone else when we get depressed, we will not be certain of God's presence. If someone else has to tell us how to face a crisis, we can never learn to look to God in faith.

Without firsthand faith, we will never experience the reality of the faith of those spiritual giants of whom it was said, "The world was not worthy of them" (Heb. 11:38). If we never meet God in a vital, life-changing way, we will not have the radiance, unselfishness, and victory that we see in people who really walk with God. Those of us who have a secondhand faith are incomplete in that we never experience what Hudson Taylor called "the exchanged life." Paul described "the exchanged life" in Galatians 2:19–20: "I have been crucified with Christ; and I no longer live, but Christ lives in me. The life I now live in the flesh, I live by faith in the Son of God, who loved me and gave Himself for me."

The Option of Firsthand Faith

Firsthand faith involves a personal encounter with God. As Job journeyed through his tragic experiences he moved into a direct relationship with God. "Now my eyes have seen You," he said (Job 42:5). Job, who began his journey defending the traditional doctrines about God and His involvement with humans, entered a new spiritual dimension when he himself saw God. Notice that Job did not find God until he lost his possessions, his children were taken from him, his body was covered with sores, his wife turned against him, and his friends castigated him. Only when Job turned away from everything he held dear did he have his personal encounter with God.

Personal encounters with God are unusual during times of prosperity—perhaps because we seldom seek Him in good times. Prosperity has a way of clouding our vision and fogging the image of God. It tends to distort our sense of dependence and give us an illusion of self-reliance. Adversity, on the other hand, tends to blow the fog away and remove the film from our eyes. When we are driven to turn to God for help in times of adversity, we see God more clearly than in times of prosperity when we do not sense our need for Him.

We do not need to wait for adversity to come before we enter into a vital, personal relationship with God. We do not have to wait until we are in desperate straits before we realize that we need God. As we sit in the comfort of prosperity and reflect upon our freedoms, we can seek an encounter with the Lord. By turning to Jesus Christ right now, we can take the decisive step to triumphant firsthand faith.

Job's Choice

When Job chose the option of firsthand faith, he repented. The word *repent* means "to change one's mind and purpose." The Hebrew word *nicham* translated "repent" in Job 42:6 is translated "comfort" in numerous other Old Testament passages. An example is Genesis 24:67, which says that "Isaac was comforted after his mother's death." So when we truly repent, we are genuinely comforted. The comfort, peace, and grace that we long to experience become ours the moment we repent and turn to God. When we repent, we open the door for God to bless us. What a beautiful choice Job made.

A New Direction

When Job repented, he turned around in his direction and purpose. His turn, however, did not result in self-hatred. The intention of Job was to convey a broader notion than self-rejection. He was not merely saying he was disappointed in himself. He was saying, "I hate everything I see in me."

Job repented of things he had done, said, and thought. He repented of the curse he had pronounced on the day of his birth because now he knew that God did not make a mistake when he was born. Job repented of his desire to die. He repented of the complaints he had made against God during his depression and despair. He repented of his rash challenges to God because now he knew that his statements were made from too limited a perspective.

When Job repented, he emptied himself and changed his direction and purpose. He bowed himself before God and let out all the venom that was stored up within his soul.

When we face the truth about ourselves, stop trusting man's ideas, and express faith in God, we are demonstrating repentance. We turn in another direction: God becomes our new objective. We change our mind and our purpose. We rely on God instead of on our own resources. Like the believers at Thessalonica, we turn "from idols to serve the living and true God" (1 Thess. 1:9). When we do that, we know God is pleased, for He affirmed Job when he repented (Job 42:7).

Job declared his faith in God and acknowledged his own inadequacy. Then he saw God. Likewise when we repent, we can expect to encounter God. Conversely, if we would see God, we need to repent. And continued repentance always follows closely behind an encounter with God. Repentance is a lifelong experience of turning from ourselves to God. We must do that daily.

Repentance involves recognizing the true nature of sin. Sin is rebellion against God's known will—against what He tells us to be and do. We sin because we want to remove God from our lives; we want to eliminate God from our reasoning. We feel that when God is out of the way, we will have no law to curb us, for there will be no Holy Spirit to keep us from doing what we want to do. Sin is directed against God. Other people may suffer when we sin, but they are not the target of our sin. Sin is first and foremost an affront to God.

When the prodigal son came home after dishonoring his father, he said, "Father, I have sinned against heaven and in your sight. I'm no longer worthy to be called your son" (Luke 15:21). After committing immorality with Bathsheba, killing Uriah, and disgracing his position as the religious and political leader of his nation, David said to the Lord, "Against You Alone I have sinned and done this evil in Your sight" (Ps. 51:4). When we come to understand that our sin is not just a shame or something we ought to regret, but an attack on God, we approach the point where we can have a personal encounter with God.

A New Standard

Before he repented, Job was always comparing himself to his friends. He argued that they were no better than he was. After he repented, God became the standard by which he measured his life.

Comparing ourselves to others is always futile because we are all sinful (Rom. 3:10; Isa. 53:6). It is no consolation to know that we are as bad as others are. As Romans 3:23 says, "All have sinned and fall short of the glory of God." And what is the glory of God? Jesus! Jesus Christ is the measure to which we compare our lives. The standard is high, for Paul wrote, "For this reason God also highly exalted Him and gave Him the name that is above every name, so that at the name of Jesus every knee should bow—of those who are in heaven and on earth and under the earth and every tongue should confess that Jesus Christ is Lord, to the glory of God the Father" (Phil. 2:9–11).

In our own power we will never measure up to Jesus Christ—no matter how many good things we have done, no matter how great others think we are, no matter how moral we are, no matter how much honesty and integrity we demonstrate, no matter how much we achieve in this world. We can never be like Him in our own strength. Compared to Jesus Christ, we all fall drastically short of the glory of God.

When Job's faith became firsthand, he acknowledged that God, not man, was the measure of his life. Like Job, we must always look to God. Jesus Christ is the standard by which we will be measured, and the only way we can measure up to His standard is to come to Him by faith. We will never measure up just by trying to be good, for we can never be good in God's sight. God's righteousness is different from ours. Scripture says, "All of us have become like something unclean, and all our righteous acts are like a polluted garment" (Isa. 64:6). God is the only one who can give us His kind of purity and righteousness.

When we choose the option of firsthand faith and come to God in repentance, we will establish a personal relationship with Him. When we thus discover God, we will discover the answer to every question of our hearts and revel in the glory of His presence. Resting on the basic premise of faith in God, we will understand Augustine's words: "Thou hast created us for thyself, and our heart cannot be quieted till it may find repose in thee."[1]

Endnotes

1 *The Confessions of St. Augustine* (trans. Watts) 1.1.

Chapter 17

The Prayer that Brings Blessing

Job 42:10

"This is not the end. It is not even the beginning of the end. But it is, perhaps, the end of the beginning."[1] These words spoken by Winston Churchill on November 10, 1942, also describe Job's experience after his encounter with the Lord. When Job met the Lord personally, he reached the end of himself and repented. In Job 42 we witness that turning point in Job's life. We also witness the moment of his release from affliction and the time of blessing that followed. It was the time when all his questions were answered by the presence of the Lord.

When Job quit trying to understand his circumstances and quit demanding an answer to his problems—when he quit struggling with his captivity and began to repent—he came to the turning point in his life. The change came when he saw a true picture of the Lord and a true picture of himself. When Job saw the Lord in all His splendor, he saw his own insignificance and repented, saying: "I had heard rumors about You, but now my eyes have seen You. Therefore I take back my words and repent in dust and ashes" (Job 42:5–6).

This pattern is repeated throughout scripture. When Isaiah saw the Lord high and lifted up, he saw a true picture of himself and his world. Then he repented: "Woe is me, for I am ruined because I am a man of unclean lips and live among a people of unclean lips" (Isa. 6:5). Moses reached a turning point when he came face to face with the very presence of God in the burning bush (Exod. 3–4). Saul (Paul) changed the direction of his life when he had a personal encounter with the Lord on the Damascus road (Acts 9).

Job reached a turning point, but there will be no turning point for us as long as we cling to our own ideas and go our own way. There will be no turning point as long as we are in rebellion against God. There will be no turning point as long as we do not repent. But if we fix our eyes on the Lord, we will gain an awareness of our unworthiness, and repentance must follow that awareness. When we reach that turning point, we experience the acceptance of the Lord. Jesus said, "Everyone the Father gives Me will come to Me, and the one who comes to Me I will never cast out" (John 6:37).

Job 42:10 speaks of the change in Job's life, and the truth of this strategic verse could revolutionize our lives as well: "After Job had prayed for his friends, the Lord restored his prosperity and doubled his previous possessions." The New International Version says, "The Lord made him prosperous again." The King James Version says, "The Lord turned the captivity of Job"; in other words, everything that was captured from Job was restored.

Freedom from Captivity

When the Lord turned the captivity of Job, he set Job free from everything that had bound up his heart and his mind. The Lord set Job free from his captivity. This does not mean the Lord set Job free from poverty, although he had lost everything. It does not mean that the Lord set Job free from sickness, although his body had been covered with boils. It does not mean that the Lord set Job free from bearing reproach. He had been accused by his friends. It does not mean that the Lord set Job free from being the target of slander. He had been misrepresented. It does not mean that the Lord set Job free from his grief. The death of his children had broken his heart. It does not mean that the Lord set Job free from discouragement. He had suffered disappointments. The Lord did more. He set Job free from being bound up in his troubles. The Lord set Job himself free.

Job's mind and heart had been in bondage. He had been captured by his circumstances, his affliction, his persecution, and his depression. Job was in bondage to everything in his life. His personal losses simply reflected the things that held him captive.

Sometimes trouble is like tar. The more we try to free ourselves from it, the more we get wrapped up in it. Job's losses held him in that kind of bondage. He struggled with grief over his children being killed, despair over losing his possessions, and hurt caused by the slander of his friends and by the disrespect of his wife. But Job's worst struggle was with the fact that his heart and mind were held captive by all the things of life.

Many of us today live under this kind of captivity. Controlled by what happens to us, we find ourselves all bound up in our adversities. When we suffer loss, we allow the circumstances of life and the cruelty of those around us to make us bitter, angry, and resentful. Then our hearts and minds are taken into bondage by these emotions. The person who makes us angry becomes the one who controls us.

Hebrews 12:14–15 says, "Pursue peace with everyone, and holiness without it no one will see the Lord. See to it that no one falls short of the grace of God and that no root of bitterness springs up, causing trouble and by it, defiling many." Bitterness grows like a poisonous plant. Once it takes root, we are held hostage to our bitterness. The object of our bitterness—whether it is a person, thing, or circumstance—is really our captor.

However pious or upright Job may have been, he was held in captivity until the Lord set him free. Many people today are held captive by their possessions or their circumstances. Others, having no joy in their faith and no excitement about their relationship with Jesus Christ, are in spiritual bondage. Only God can set them free. The Lord stands ready to release us.

> He breaks the power of canceled sin,
> He sets the prisoner free;
> His blood can make the foulest clean;
> His blood availed for me.[2]

The good news is that there was an end to Job's captivity, and there can be an end to ours too. His night of sorrow and grief ceased; the winter of his oppression and disappointment did not last forever. Satan was defeated in Job's personal experience, and he can be defeated in ours. God was glorified in Job's life, and He can be glorified in ours. Whatever we are going through, God will accompany us. If we keep our eyes on the Lord, a time of release will come. In the meantime He will give us peace and victory in the midst of our difficulties.

Notice that Job's release from captivity was conditional: "After Job had prayed for his friends, the Lord restored his prosperity and doubled his previous possessions." The Lord restored Job's losses "*after* he prayed for his friends" (Job 42:10, italics added). *After* "the Lord accepted Job's prayer" (Job 42:9, italics added), He gave him the assignment of intercession.

Assignment of Intercession

With acceptance from the Lord, Job's life was at the end of its beginning. His life from this point on would radiate the goodness and blessing of the Lord. Before his losses were restored, however, he had to pray for his friends who had been so confrontational toward him. He did not receive the benefits of his repentance until he expressed God's attitude toward those who had dealt him so much misery. God waited until Job reflected his heart's transformation in intercessory prayer for those who had been so unkind toward him. That is exactly what Jesus did on the cross! He prayed, "Father, forgive them, because they do not know what they are doing" (Luke 23:34).

Job prayed for his critics. He lifted his slanderous friends up before the Lord in intercessory prayer. His friends had falsely accused him of self-seeking and self-righteousness. They had misrepresented him and questioned his motives. Their attitudes, actions, and theology had been wrong. But instead of returning the kind of vicious attack he had received, Job prayed for his arrogant, rebellious friends.

Eliphaz, Zophar, and Bildad were pompous and abusive in the extreme, but Job prayed for them. The Lord said He would not accept their prayers, so Job interceded for his powerless friends before the throne of grace.

We need to follow the example of Job and carry our rebellious friends to the Lord in prayer. Even if they slander us, we do not need to talk about them over the telephone. If we spent more time talking to God about them, we will be astounded at the difference it will make. We free ourselves from the bondage of bitterness and resentment when we pray for the person who caused those emotions.

When we, like Job, experience the forgiveness of God, we cannot do anything less than forgive those who have wronged us. When our hearts are transformed by the Lord, we are able to love those who have done us wrong. We are capable of loving others because He first loved us (1 John 4:19).

The blessings that were bestowed when Job prayed for his friends were acts of grace. Both he and his friends were given something they did not deserve. God did not honor Job because of his righteous character.

God's gracious act of restoring Job's blessings was triggered by Job's gracious act of interceding for his friends. Job's restoration coincided with his prayer of intercession. When he prayed for his friends, "The Lord gave Job twice as much as he had before."

Privilege of Intercession

There is nothing nobler than to pray for other people, especially those who may not be able to pray effectively for themselves. Intercessory prayer is one of the greatest privileges of our lives.

Intercessory Prayer for Our Children

Abraham prayed for his son Ishmael. "Abraham said to God, 'If only Ishmael could live in Your presence!' But God said, 'No. Your wife Sarah will bear you a son, and you will name him Isaac. I will confirm My covenant with him as an everlasting covenant for his offspring after him. As for Ishmael, I have heard you. I will certainly bless him; I will make him fruitful and will multiply him greatly ... I will make him into a great nation'" (Gen. 17:18–20). God promised to bless Ishmael, and so the Arab nations of today are his descendants. Just as Abraham interceded for his children, we ought to intercede for ours. They should be constantly in our thoughts and prayers.

Intercessory Prayer for the Lost

Abraham also prayed for Sodom and Gomorrah. He pleaded with God to spare those wicked cities if even ten righteous people could be found there. The Lord destroyed the cities but sent angels to rescue Abraham's nephew, Lot. Today we should intercede for the crime-ridden, drug-filled streets of America. What a difference we could make if we would pray for the lost people in this land and throughout the world. We need to remember the power of prayer that God has given to us.

Intercessory Prayer for Our Nation

Moses prayed for the nation of Israel when God was ready to judge it (Num. 14:11–15). We ought to pray for our nation and the secular leaders of our world. Proverbs 21:1 declares, "A king's heart is a water channel in the Lord's hand: He directs it whenever He chooses." Paul instructed young Timothy, "First of all, then, I urge that petitions, prayers, intercessions, and thanksgivings be made for everyone, for kings and all those who are in authority so that we may lead a tranquil and quiet life in all godliness and dignity."

Intercessory Prayer for One Another

It is our privilege and responsibility to pray for one another. We should echo the words Samuel addressed to Israel: "I vow that I will not sin against the Lord by ceasing to pray for you" (1 Sam. 12:23). Our Lord interceded for His disciples (see His great high priestly prayer in John 17) and Paul interceded for believers (see Eph. 1:16; 3:14–19). And the apostle Paul also asked believers to pray for him and his coworkers (2 Thess. 3:1). The writer of Hebrews made a similar request (Heb. 13:18–19). Since trials and testings come frequently, we should pray regularly for one another. Just as we schedule regular times to eat in order to sustain ourselves physically, we ought to schedule regular times to pray in order to sustain ourselves spiritually.

Intercessory Prayer for Our Enemies

Jesus said, "I tell you, love your enemies and pray for those who persecute you" (Matt. 5:44). Jesus prayed for His enemies on the cross (Luke 23:34). Following the teaching and example of Jesus, we should pray for those who revile and persecute us. When Stephen was martyred for preaching the gospel, he followed the example of Jesus. As his enemies stoned him, Stephen "knelt down and cried out with a loud voice, 'Lord, do not charge them with this sin!'" (Acts 7:60).

It is easy to pray for our children, our friends, and those who love us, but it is difficult to pray for our enemies. To pray for those who oppose what we stand for is not natural. We cannot do it on our own strength. The Lord must be moving in our lives to enable us to pray for those who attack us.

Job's life turned around when he prayed for his friends. When we become people of prayer, God will turn our lives around, too. When we learn the secret of praying for others, whether they are friends or foes, God will release us from whatever or whoever holds us in bondage.

The blessing of God will rain down on our lives when we become intercessors, praying for everyone the Lord brings to our minds. As we pray for the people God places before us, our Christian lives will become more joyful. When we start to intercede for others, we will discover that our spiritual lives are not at their end, nor at the beginning of the end, but at the end of their beginning.

Endnotes

1 Winston Churchill, *Familiar Quotations by John Bartlett* (Boston: Little, Brown & Co., 13th ed.) 871a.
2 From the hymn "O for a Thousand Tongues" by Charles Wesley.